P.S.
Burn
This
Letter
Please

P.S. Burn This Letter Please

The fabulous and fraught birth of modern drag, in the queens' own words

CRAIG OLSEN

SPHERE

SPHERE

First published in Great Britain in 2023 by Sphere

1 3 5 7 9 10 8 6 4 2

Copyright © Craig Olsen 2023
Extracts from letters © Richard Konigsberg, President of the Edward F. Limato
Foundation. Reproduced with permission.

The moral right of the author has been asserted.

A CIP catalogue record for this book
is available from the British Library.

HB ISBN 978-0-7515-8594-0
C format ISBN 978-0-7515-8592-6

Typeset in Bodoni by M Rules
Printed and bound in Great Britain by
Clays Ltd, Elcograf S.p.A.

Papers used by Sphere are from well-managed forests
and other responsible sources.

Sphere
An imprint of
Little, Brown Book Group
Carmelite House
50 Victoria Embankment
London EC4Y 0DZ

An Hachette UK Company
www.hachette.co.uk

www.littlebrown.co.uk

For Ed and Billy, Robbie and Richie, my chosen family, who have shown me the true meaning of love and acceptance. And to all the brave queens who have inspired us with their resilience and fearlessness in being their authentic selves, this book is dedicated to you.

JAN RICHARDS

TERI NOEL

CHRIS AMES

SANDY ROGERS

HANS CRYSTAL

VICKIE LYNN

Contents

List of Illustrations

Introduction

Thank goddess that these letters weren't burned. I'm certain that many others were. Others may be buried in boxes, waiting to be found and pieced together, like Craig has done so lovingly for these. If he hadn't had that glimmer of recognition and become such a caretaker of these letters, we wouldn't have the chance to fall so deeply in love with these queens of New York City past! So thank goddess for that, too. I particularly adore the snarky Daphne, "Star reporter of the NY gay set rat race," Josephine and Claudia, the queens who stole thirty-five wigs from the Met Opera, and Robin Tyler, the "dyke drag queen" who performed as Judy Garland at Club 82 . . . but there are so many others in these pages.

Personal accounts like these are necessary for queer history. They are an antidote to the depressing "official record": the newspaper articles, psychiatric reports, and police archives that often try to paint queer expression (and drag in particular) as a trend, a shock, a tragedy, or worse. Instead, personal ephemera—letters, snapshots, stories—reveal the greater truth: the simple beauty of living life on one's own terms!

We don't just need drag "icons"—activists written into history and superstars immortalized in pop culture. We need "ordinary" queens too: the ones who made their splash and then retired, the

ones who were a little too anxious to raise their voices for revolution, the ones who just wanted to find love, the ones who were lost too soon. In some ways it's easier to recognize yourself in that kind of story: slangy, self-effacing, horny, overly ambitious, insecure, shady, and oh so human. In other words: totally normal, like all of us.

The letters in this collection come from the particularly conservative 1950s and 60s in New York City. Despite official laws banning homosexuality and drag, queer life in this era is surprisingly well-documented. Scholars like Esther Newton (*Mother Camp*, 1972), Roger Baker (*Drag*, 1968), and Martin Duberman (*Stonewall*, 1993) published interviews with "street queens," "professional impersonators," and everything in between. Underground magazines from the era like *Transvestia* (1960) or *Female Mimics* (1963) offer stunning first-hand accounts of activism and artistry alike. Because of the proliferation of these incredible stories, and also the challenging conditions faced in real life, drag from this era has grown particularly inspiring to today's generation of drag queens and kings, myself included! It reminds us where we come from, and illuminates some of the political inequalities that still remain.

But the collection of letters in this book nevertheless reveals a fresh angle to this already vital picture—a joy and messiness that we must always remember. These young queens are silly and gossipy and sometimes a little superficial, and that's a part of life! Several of the figures in this story did go on to blaze trails—like Robin Tyler, who became an activist in the 70s or Terry "Teri" Noel, a drag queen who used mafia connections to secretly transition in the 60s. But others, like the central recipient of the letters, Ed or "Reno"—lived a more quiet life, utilizing certain privileges to build wealth and success while largely losing touch with the community (although he did keep the letters, a bittersweet reminder of his big queer youth).

Without a doubt, though, no one in this story is a classic hero . . . and that's part of what makes it so interesting. After all, the most striking thing about these letters is not how the writers detail their struggles or victories, but how they simply joked and expressed joy with each other, looking past changing circumstances to forge real community (even a temporary one). And let's not forget the most important takeaway: that no matter what, we should always remember to camp, carry, and pull a scene! Kisses, darling, got to go!

Xxx

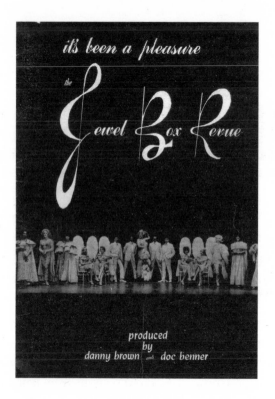

it's been a pleasure

the Jewel Box Revue

produced
by
danny brown and doc benner

In their Own Words

For drag queens—as for any marginalized group—history is not always valued or deemed worthy of preservation. Because of this lack of access to primary evidence, historians have been forced to rely on alternative accounts, such as arrest records and hospital admissions. Personal letters, journals, and diaries were destroyed and burned upon request of the writer, or by a member of their family, who discovered they were different. If there was no proof, there was no crime.

The resilience of LGBTQ+ people during the twentieth century was without doubt impressive and the lengths they went to in order for their identities to remain hidden were radical. As a result of their need for secrecy, these queens developed an extraordinary lexicon of their own. It likely served both as a queer shorthand while simultaneously protecting their conversations from being understood from an outsider. These words and phrases, sprinkled throughout the letters, fascinate me. It was a thrill to rediscover some of these forgotten terms that fell out of fashion between the 1950s and finding the letters. Even more amazingly, however, some of the catchphrases are still in rotation today.

Isn't that a flip?!

Bamboola Glamazon	over the top Glamazon
bar rag	a person who frequents bars often
batz	insane
boomataza	Italian word for hooker
bummy/bummish	stylish, attractive, sophisticated
cracked	taken off guard, surprised. "When I saw that beauty, I cracked."
the end scene	the absolute best
face scene	the way a person looks
fach	face
a flip	a funny or ironic situation; enthusiastic. "What a flip!" "I flipped over it."
full face	a complete and polished makeup look
john	a male companion who pays for sex
Mehroned	Mehron has been a brand of makeup since 1927
mopping	the act of stealing or having sex
nell	an effeminate male
next	over it
nube	someone new to the scene
paint	to apply makeup to the face
pancake scene	heavily made up
pink tea	women's bathroom
pulling a scene	pulling something off convincingly or to get away with
rube	unsophisticated person
steak dinner	a guy who will buy dinner for you
stell	a muscular guy
stip	heels
trade	straight or straight-acting homosexual male
tea room	bathroom

It is also worth noting that when decoding the language, a word or phrase can take on different meanings dependent on context. For example, "Pulling a scene" has three different connotations:

"The biggest dish around town is drag. I mopped on a platinum white wig. It's a cap wig but the hair is long and the end. It costs one fifty. Baker took me to a place, and we pulled the scene."

"Pulled the scene" here refers to stealing/mopping.

"She wants me to have it worked on. It needs a little adding on the bottom for the 'Jayne' look. I'm still debating whether to pull a scene."

"Pull a scene" here refers to the drag scene.

"The fags are going all out this year. Many beaded sheaths and things. If I can't pull the end scene, I'm not pulling any at all."

"Pull the end scene" here refers to being the absolute best.

Language – and spelling – were used playfully, and were constantly evolving, reflecting the lives of the queens who used this code. Although it can be challenging to unpack the context, the flexibility of the vernacular is part of its charm.

CHAPTER ONE

A Discovery of Queens

The evening was unusually warm after an afternoon rain in Los Angeles during the spring of 2014. Earthquake weather. I pulled the car up to my garage and waited for the faux wood door to raise. I had just finished a long, full day at the office with clients and was looking forward to a relaxing evening on the sofa in front of the television with the dogs. The automatic door lifted, and I quickly realized my evening plans were about to change. Scattered around the garage were dozens of brown cardboard packing boxes, stacked one atop the other, with the name LIMATO scrawled across them in handwritten capital letters.

My close friend of two decades, Edward F. Limato, one of the biggest and brightest Hollywood super-agents, died seven days before his seventy-fourth birthday in 2010. My partner Richard was assigned the daunting task of executor of his late mentor's estate. This arduous process required liquidating three homes and nearly every possession Ed owned. Now the estate was closed and the last of this man's extraordinary life was reduced to what was in these boxes; belongings and ephemera that included Ed's personal documents, letters, photo albums, and private journals. Blockbuster movie posters behind cracked glass in black metal frames starring actors from his stable of A-List celebrities. His antiquated "old school" Rolodex neatly storing the phone numbers of every major player in Hollywood typed out on white cards. Trunks filled with curiosities, including a collection of vintage matchbooks from dinner clubs and bars around the world. Copies of faxes and phone records from the early years up to his final days, with notes regarding what the topic of conversation was, scrawled in red ink. These items were a few of many among the potpourri of contents.

Although he wasn't a hoarder, Ed was certainly a documentarian of his own life and times; a life that was contained in over fifty boxes now stacked to the rafters.

The storage pod had been sitting in a dark, airconditioned warehouse somewhere in Los Angeles for the past four years, and I had inconveniently forgotten that we had scheduled the drop off for today. Damnit! Now began the final job: going through each box with the primary purpose of throwing the unnecessary, unsentimental, or uninteresting items into the trash. Staring up at the cardboard towers I felt immediately overwhelmed and defeated, dreading the work that lay ahead. In that moment my real motivation was to clear a path and get my car in the garage. I rolled up my sleeves and yanked down a box at random. Secretly, I hoped I would find something inexplicable. Who wouldn't? That would the exciting part of all this.

I opened the first box and pulled out a piece of stationery with the letterhead: THE DEPARTMENT OF TRANSPORTATION, dated October 5 1957 and addressed to a person named Reno Martin. As I skimmed the letter, I couldn't have known how significant a discovery this would become.

Nov 5, 1951

Dear Reno—

Baker got me all hopped up on drag again. We were having coffee at the Waldorf about 4 o'clock. Some butch looking rube comes over and asks us if we know where "you can get big size high heels." Well that immediately set the drag ball rolling. We were sitting with this psychiatrist number we met in the bar. Much the eye-glass number. A scene for me like. He's going to be there tonight. He comes from Ireland and said he's making a study of "characters" like ourselves. Very nice though! Bought us drinks and everything. He was giving us the whole dish on the gay scene in the old Greek times. — I'm sure I was born in the wrong era. — I think I would have mopped much more in a toga than nell pink tea pants. The scene was really on in those days!

I saw Kim Drawback. She says hello. She gained a little weight. She's trying to like crazy "to get that Kim effect." She's crazy. Josephine told me that "Frankie's pulling" the drag scene this year in an all-out comeback number. But it seems to me I've heard that song before! Seeing is believing. I wasn't bothered about drag until Jo started bugging my ass. And Billy wasn't bothered until I started bugging her ass on the phone just now. I'll definitely give Baker your address tonight. I always forget to bring it. According to Josephine the drag is supposed to be a whopper this year. But then again they always say that. I heard so many versions of who's wearing what. You never know what they're wearing until they show up. And neither do they. I have a couple of very "yamyambambensteinish" ideas. But with Billy so unsettled and everything I don't know what the story will be. She doesn't know herself.

I remain—

As always—

Daphne

October 5, 1957

Dear Reno,

Baker got me all hopped up on drag again. We were having coffee at the Waldorf about 4 o'clock. Some butch looking rube comes over and asks us if we know where "you can get big size high heels." Well, that immediately set the drag ball rolling. We were sitting with this physiatrist number, we met in the bar. Much the eye glass number. A scene for me like. He's going to be there tonight. He comes from Ireland and said he's making a study of "characters" like ourselves. Very nice though! Bought us drinks and everything. He was giving us the whole dish on the gay scene in the old Greek times. I'm sure I was born in the wrong era. I think I would have mopped much more in a toga than nell pink tea pants. The scene was really on in those days! ... According to Josephine the drag is supposed to be a whopper this year. But then again, they always say that. I heard so many versions of who's wearing what. You never know what they're wearing until they show up. And neither do they. I have a couple of very "zambam- binsteemish" ideas. But with Billy so unsettled and everything I don't know what the story will be. She doesn't know herself.

I remain, As Always,
Daphne

... Where you can get big size high heels ...
... According to Josephine the drag is supposed to be a whopper this year ...

Drag? What? My interest was piqued! I pulled out another letter dated 1958, then another, 1955 and another, 1957. There was over two hundred letters in this box alone from many different authors, predominantly female. Even though some were handwritten, others neatly typed, some on proper stationery and others scrawled across random pieces of paper, they all had one thing in common—all were addressed to Reno Martin. Who was Reno? My heart was racing as I read another letter.

Dear Reno: Nov. 19-1957

Well that scene flipped me about
that trade hitchhiking, It sounds just
perfect. Sooo you're still looking for
romance eh! well the scene is ogk
forget about it theres no happiness for a fagg.

The scene in New York is very but
very _stale_. and I mean everything trade
& all. nobody is mopping really that
much Dapne stays home, Billy disapeared
from the scene camille Hybronated, so
far the only ones that are mopping is
gigi + Frankie (But they mop 4 times a day
all year around) anyway. Georgie went for
her licence at the State Board - I think
she made it. Tony L. had a fight with
Kaiva & shes back on the scene over
gigi. well as far as me Im so fucking
tied up in that cursed school I come
home at 7.30 and I have no feeling for
anything nor energy to go cruising so
I mopp on weekends mostly, I cant wait
to finish that coarse Im almost there
a couple of months & Ill be thru.
"Thank God". so Dish how long have you
been gone now? you should have saved
all your loot in the Bank. theres much
Shit going on with Algene so I wont
see her for a while.

I mopped today with Caldonia - you
know that store on Park Ave & 51st "Dominique
France" for men well anyway it was
sensational I walked in the door were all
opened I picked out 4 gorgeous sweaters
& flew out. Cal flipped she was waiting out
side she died! the sweaters cost from $55 to
75 all gorgeous (Red. White. Grey, Brown & blk)
the white one is Fabalous a big criss cross
collar doorman sleves, the red & grey are like
that black one I sold Dapne for $10.00 remember??
tell what a scene... Im starting my winter
collection already.

Love   Jo Baker

November 19, 1957

Dear Reno:

So you're still looking for romance eh! Well, the scene is off forget about it there's no happiness for a fagg. I mopped today— you know that store on Park Avenue and 51st St., Dominique France, well anyway it was so sensational. I walked in the door were all opened I picked out 4 gorgeous sweaters and flew out. The sweaters cost from $55 to $75 all gorgeous (red, white, gray, brown + black) Well what a scene ... I'm starting my winter collection already.

Love,

Jo Baker

The writers shared a common language which I found hard to decipher. The slang they used was fascinating and foreign to me. The themes discussed were salacious and exciting—romance, sex work, crime—and I could only imagine how much more shocking these topics would have been in the New York of the 1950s.

The letters were candid and honest, and I began to wonder if I should be reading them at all? The interior lives of the writers were exposed, and I was not the intended recipient of these missives. But it wasn't as though I had stolen my sister's diary; I didn't know these people—and what was the alternative? Throw them away? So, I gave myself permission, convincing myself it was alright, and I would just read a few more ...

Several hours later, I sat in the kitchen with my partner Richard, letters placed one on top of another and several more scattered around the table.

I was hooked. I found myself laughing and sometimes crying over the monologues these writers shared with Reno. I could see the letters coming to life in my mind like scenes in a movie, as the writers regaled Reno with stories from the days, evenings or weeks before.

It was a puzzle, but as I studied more of these documents, I began putting the pieces together, over the course of that evening. I was delighted to learn the letter writers were indeed a cliquish group of drag queens! Joe, GiGi, Billie, Charlie, Josephine and Daphne, young rebellious queens who called themselves the Boomatzas. Their personal lives intertwined with one another, and they held nothing back when dishing to Reno. These writers' ambitions were recognizable to me. I keenly felt their desire to fit in, to belong, to love and be loved, and their longing to be accepted by a world that could be, by all accounts, unbearably cruel.

I heard a voice in the back of my mind, "You found them!" and then it hit me: the records I held in my hands shone a light on this group of young men's lives and captured their voices at a specific time in history I knew absolutely nothing about. Queer people living their lives and dressing in drag in New York City during the 1950s? I thought I knew everything there was to know about queer culture. Clearly, I did not! But this answer only precipitated more questions.

Who was Reno Martin? Why did Ed save these letters, addressed to a stranger, safe and secret for decades? I had to know!

The Ed Limato *I* knew wasn't a fan of drag. He wanted nothing to do with it and had made that clear on many occasions. I remembered a specific Friday night, sitting in the living room at Ed's home in Beverly Hills, listening to a new artist Elton John had discovered named Duffy. Ed's Friday nights were always something to look forward to. This particular evening, I was carrying a recent Polaroid taken of me leaning forward in the director's chair on a film set. I was in drag and completely transformed. There wasn't a hint of the "boy" in me to be seen, and I made a stunning girl (if I do say so myself)!

I passed the photo to Ed, asking, "Do you think this girl is pretty?" I posed as he studied the photo, hoping he might be about to discover a new star.

"She's a beautiful girl, Craigy. Who is she?" he asked, inquisitively.

"It's ME!" I gleefully sang out and took a bow.

He snapped back at me like a pit bull. "I don't like that kind of thing!" His deep baritone bark ruining the soft melodic tone of Duffy's vocals, "I don't like that kind of thing."

I knew I had crossed an invisible line with Ed. His emotional reaction was unnecessarily forceful. He was dead serious. I shrugged it off back then, but thinking back on that moment, it now made sense. That exchange meant more to him than I could have known. Why?

After weeks of sleuthing, I solved the first mystery. In Ed's personal belongings I found an old tape recording from his broadcasting school days, when he was training to be an announcer, in which he introduced himself as Reno Martin. Reno Martin and Ed Limato were one in the same.

Standing there, proud after making the connection, I realized that this discovery opened a Pandora's box of further mysteries. I had been friends with Ed for years; why did he have an alias, and what was he hiding? I was determined to have my questions answered.

Reno Martin was the stage name Ed gave himself during his days as a young disk jockey in New Orleans. After pondering the choice of alias, eventually a light went off in my mind. Years before, Ed and I had watched a golden age musical in his screening room, *Anything Goes*. Two of the lead characters names were Reno Sweeney and Moonface Martin. Ed once told me a successful film must have the girl every woman wants to be and the man every guy wants to be. Ed had combined the names of the two characters and became Reno Martin! Reno was the beloved ringleader of this group of young and very rebellious queens who called themselves the Boomatzas.

Although Ed never spoke of these letters or this time in his life, looking back, I'm convinced he wanted me to discover them. "You found them, kid." I would hear Ed's deep voice repeating over and over in the back of my mind. "You found them!"

Sept 9, 1957

Dear Reno

The other night I met
Richard, and he happened to have
the letter you wrote him. Naturally
I read it and thought you had
some nerve telling him that
we were fighting to see who
will be the Star. I know
that you were gone, thats
all you ever think of. Believe
me "baby" thats not the way
I look at it. Just because your
away do you think I am trying
to take over, "You Crazy" How
could you even think such a
thing like that of me, as
soon as I read the letter
I come home, and started to
write this letter at 2 o'clock in
the morning, thats how mad
I was. I am not mopping that
other because of the cops are
always on our necks. And
another thing I was amazed
about was you saying that
Mount Vernon was all yours, Nobody
is trying to take your place, I
do alright as Charlie I am
getting very sleepy so I'll close
Ya Know.

Your Friend
Always.
Charlie

Love + Kisses
x x x x x x

Sept 9, 1957

Dear Reno

The other nite I met Richard, and he happened to have the letter you wrote him. Naturally I read it and thought you had some nerve telling him that you were fighting to see who will be the "star" now that you were gone, that's all you ever think of. Believe [me] "baby" that's not the way I look at it, just because you're away do you think I am anything to take over, "Your Crazy" How could you even think such a thing like that of me, as soon as I read the letter I came home, and started to write this letter at 2 o'clock in the morning, that's how mad I was. I was not mopping that often because of the cops are always on our necks. And another thing I was annoyed about was you saying that Mount Vernon was all yours, nobody is trying to take your place, I do alright as "Charlie". I am getting very sleepy so I'll close for know.

Your friend always
Charlie

Ed had trusted me to be the custodian of these letters, handing me the baton after protecting them himself for the majority of his adult life. I could only guess that my background was the reason why. I was the result of a successful first date. Born in 1969, in the same month Neil Armstrong took his first small step on the moon, my father did what any good midwestern Christian man should and married my mother in a shotgun wedding. My mother was recently divorced with two little girls from her previous marriage. I was number three. Not quite *The Brady Bunch*.

From a very young age, I knew I wasn't like anyone else, and the day it was confirmed is still imprinted on my memory. Sitting on the floor in front of the television, watching Bert and Ernie on *Sesame Street*, the doorbell rang, and I hopped up to answer it. Our neighbor Geri came over to borrow a cup of sugar. (They used to do that back in the 70s bored housewives would find any excuse to hang out with other bored housewives when their husbands were away at work.)

Geri lived across the street. Under her arm she carried a Sears catalogue she opened to ask my mother her opinion on a dress. Geri placed the heavy book on the orange Formica dining table; it was as thick as a bible, the only other heavy book I knew anything about. She poured herself a cup of coffee, sat down with my mother and they both lit a cigarette.

The two were chatting, their voices fading into the background as I pulled the heavy catalogue to my side of the table and began to look through all the pages. I especially loved the toy section, which was followed by children's apparel. I turned a page and noticed this pretty little black girl wearing a red knee-length coat with big white pom poms as buttons. Her black hair was combed down the middle and she had two pigtails, like my sisters would wear. She had on white tights and flat shiny white shoes with a little strap that went across the top of her foot. I remember thinking she was the prettiest little girl I had ever seen.

"Whatcha doin' over there?" my mother asked.

"Nothing," I replied.

"He likes to shop, that one!" Geri proclaimed. Smiling at me she continued, "Hey, what do you want to be when you grow up? Huh? Do you want to be a fireman? Do you want to do what your daddy does?"

I had no idea what my daddy did. My mother chimed in, "Craig, what do you want to be when you grow up? Answer Geri."

I looked up at their faces staring back at me and without hesitation, I put my finger on the smiling, happy little girl in the red coat and said, "I want to be her. I want to be her when I grow up."

They shot a look to each other, and the room suddenly went still. The only movement was a thin trail of cigarette smoke dancing past my mother's stare. That was the moment. The moment I realized I was different, and others could see it too. From that moment on everything in my life got harder. I now understood what it was like to be judged. I became aware at almost five years old I had said the wrong thing and could sense my mother's shame.

Raised in a conservative Christian household, my mother and father made me attend church three times a week. I didn't like church. I liked God because God loved everyone, and I was taught I was created in His image. I was also told, however, that it was a sin to be different, and this lesson felt targeted towards me personally. I wasn't trying to be "different," I was just being myself. Was being myself an abomination for my family to be ashamed of? Sometimes I thought that God had made a mistake and was ashamed of me too. They teach you in church God doesn't make mistakes, so why would God create me to condemn me? I was branded a "sissy boy" and bullied at school and at home by my now three sisters (yes, my parents had another accident), while my disapproving parents looked on.

As years passed, I retreated inward—both emotionally and behind the closed door of my room where being myself was neither viewed as a sin nor with shame. At night I lay in the twin bed with Bambi sheets I shared with my younger sister and listened through the thin walls to my mother crying and pleading with my father, who came home from the California Tavern drunk with increasing regularity. I would hear the door slam and the car engine revving up, then see car headlights casting shadows across the walls of my bedroom as he backed out of the driveway and drove away. Naturally, I assumed I was the reason my daddy didn't want to be home. Listening to the sobbing from the other room, I closed my eyes and I pleaded with God, to Jesus, to my Lord and Saviour, "Please make me normal." I drifted off to sleep only to wake the next morning and repeat the day before.

By the time I left for college, a closeted eighteen-year-old whose lack of self-confidence was tempered by a creative spirit and vivid imagination, I was eager to start new and leave the ghosts of my childhood behind, taking that broken little boy with me.

Early on, I befriended a tall, slight-framed boy with light eyes and blond hair. Robbie was an out and proud eighteen-year-old student in the theater program at our school, Cornish College of the Arts. He was amazing; his humor was sophisticated and witty, and he carried himself with confidence. Robbie was completely and unashamedly himself, and I admired his openness, something I was entirely too afraid to reveal—and I was going to theater school, for God's sake!

I so badly wanted to share in the fearlessness he presented to the world. It was no surprise adoration seemed to follow him everywhere.

I, on the other hand, was unable to tell my truth. My upbringing was too torturous, and I was terrified of the judgment I would undoubtedly receive from family and strangers. I knew I would never be accepted by the society in which I had been raised, so I struggled to accept myself as a result. After all, I was a Christian and that was impossible to reconcile with a gay identity. Gay? Nobody wants to be gay. But I know now that my sexuality wasn't a choice, and I simply couldn't admit the truth to myself. At twenty years of age, if I could have taken a magic pill to be, or appear as, what society considered normal, I would have taken it gladly, without hesitation.

But little by little, with Robbie's undeniable friendship and unwavering support, my confidence grew. I slowly started to find my own voice in my corner of the world. Eventually, I came out to myself and began the long road to self-acceptance.

Halloween has always been my favorite holiday. In 1991 Robbie and I planned to go out in costume to a party at a local club, Neighbors, on Capitol Hill in Seattle. I had two French courtesan costumes and one French fop costume left over from a play I had performed in. Robbie wanted to go dressed in drag as a courtesan and I, of course, would be the fop, the male equivalent. Being fresh out of the closet, I wasn't brave enough to go the distance. That evening we helped each other get ready before we hit the streets. We looked like we were straight out of *Dangerous Liaisons*.

Watching Robbie come to life that night and play in this costume (and seeing the attention he was receiving from the crowds of strangers), inspired me to be a bit braver the following evening. Emboldened, I took an old wig I had "borrowed" from the costume department at school and recreated it to replicate an authentic French style, then added a violin and two white doves nesting in the mountain of curls—I couldn't resist a touch of camp to elevate the look. I quickly discovered I was beautiful and convincing as a girl! That night was a dream as we played our parts and worked our costumes and had the crowds eating out of the palms of our hands! I was accepted. I wasn't afraid. I was celebrated. I wasn't bullied. I was admired. I wasn't ashamed.

I never looked back

After graduating, we made our way to Los Angeles as two more trained actors with the sole purpose of breaking into the business. It was the 90s and drag was by no way mainstream. Robbie and I would go out on weeknights dressed in drag and infiltrate the clubs. We created our personas to be as "real" as you could possibly get, passing unnoticed in public. Nothing to see here but two incredibly sexy, strong, confident girlfriends wearing the latest fashion going out for an evening on the town! Brooke Daniels and Taylor Michaels were hitting the scene and taking on L.A.'s nightlife. We were the 90s Girls!

Every third Saturday, we found ourselves at Drag Strip 66, a pop-up drag club at Rodolfo's in Silverlake. We would be whisked to the front of the line and never expected to pay a cover. When we walked into the club it felt as though the sea parted. It was a performance from the moment we stepped out and anyone who happened upon us became a part of the scene as we never broke character! It was a rule of ours to never break the illusion until we were behind the closed door of our apartment and only then, when the wig and pads came off, we could breathe again!

It wasn't long before we caught the eye of the Dragon Agency whose specialty was representing "odd talent." We were their lucky penny. Our agent Robin, an alternative tattooed girl with long bleach-blonde hair, would send the two of us out to audition for comic roles primarily in drag. Without fail, one of us would book the job. We worked in film and television for years as the "drag role" if a script called for it. I like to believe I got roles because I could deliver a line, but I don't want to fool myself—I looked so authentic as a girl it was hard not to be cast.

While my drag personas and performances have evolved over time, that very first spark within me was reignited when reading the letters. I believe Ed meant for me to find that box of letters because I would get a kick out of them, but I also feel he knew beyond all doubt that I would have a connection to the writers based on my interest in the artform. At first, I wasn't exactly sure what to do with the letters, but I was certain of one thing, they were not going back in the box.

After months of research in widely established LGBTQ+ archival institutions in New York, Los Angeles and San Francisco, while combing through misfiled folders, police records and photographs as well as reading and re-reading books by gay historians and authors like Esther Newton, and George Chauncy, I began to realize first-hand accounting of queer lives during this period in American history is extremely limited. Correspondence like this, by a group of drag queens sharing their lives unfiltered in New York in the 1950s, does not feature. The letters are proof of a world that was shrouded in secrecy and existed in the shadows of traditional, conservative American life. These letters were a "missing link" in our collective drag history, a body of evidence that should be documented, shared, and celebrated with the world.

The next step was hiring a private investigator to track down any of the queens from the letters. We were hopeful some of them would still be alive, though they would be well into their eighties and nineties. Of all the writers, Daphne was the most prolific and I found her letters exciting. I could feel her cleverly striking the match as she ignited a story, and I couldn't resist feeling joy when reading her salutation "As Always, Daphne" in flowery cursive.

February 7, 1958

We'll here's Hedda again giving you the latest dish! The lady is a tramp, but unlike the song, she does dish the dirt with the rest of the girls ...

As Always, Daphne

The "day to day" she curates and shares in each letter creates a visual tapestry weaving together personal moments of her life by telling a story in descriptive detail. I envisioned her writing or typing the letter at a small desk near a window in her bedroom on the

second floor of her parents' home in Queens. I didn't have a photo of
Daphne and I had no idea what she might look like, but I imagined a
beautiful girl in white with blonde hair, lidded eye, and a soft arched
brow. The essence of Daphne I constructed in my mind was Marilyn
Monroe from *How to Marry a Millionaire*.

November 20, 1957

Dear Reno,

    I had the end of end Saturday nights. I went out
despite the fact that my mother and father were up the
bronx at the wake. As usual lately when I go out on the
weekend, I pulled the suit and tie scene. And again as
usual. I went down the 415 bar. I couldn't wait to see if
my 5 & 10 beauty would show up again. Well much to my
very, very pleasant surprise, he did !
    I was thinking of how I used to watch him from acros
the counter where he worked at the 5 & 10. Of all the
times I used to go in there and have coffee or something
just for an excuse to see him. And I can't forget the
way all the Juaneenas in the store used to dish me. When
he had asked me recently why I was in there so often, I
said I was working in the Roxy show across the street at
the time. "Is that why you wore all that makeup?" Yes.
If he only knew the way I was dying to talk to him. Of
all the times I used to go out even in snowy weather, to
see if he was still working there. And of the day I
really died when I found out he wasn't anymore, and that
I might never see him again. It all seemed like a dream
now. The fact that we finally met and were sitting here
together in this romantic setting. I used to devise ways
of trying to meet him. Or even get to talk to him. I
tried once at the store. But very unsucessfully. It
seemed so hopeless. And now this ! It was really more
than I could have asked for. This was really my week of
weekends. And I could'nt forget him saying--"If you go,
I'll go."
    The John wanted us to all go
up to his apartment for drinks. Bob-"That sounds good.
Me- Gay! Nel- O really it's so Late. Me- "O don't be
a rube '. Nel- What's a rube ?   O forget it! I
figured, I'll never get her up there. And she'll never
let Bob go featuring a scene would take place. And a
scene would have been too much for me to ask for. So I
proposed that we all go for coffee.   We were all

in a cab now. The car had belonged to the other John.
We drove to 57th St where we gave the John the bar rag.
I got his telephone number. I figure he's got loot and
that he knowd many bummish people. After the cab glew
with the John in it, we went for coffee. If there was
ever a time that three was a crowd, This was definitely
it. It was more like a mob! While I had been taking the
John's number in the cab, I Heard Bob tell her " We can
both walk you home first, and then I'll walk Mike to the
subway"! No Bobby baby. We'll bothe walk Mike to the
subway first. And then we'll go Home. That Son of a
Bitch I thought. Then Bob said "Im not tired at all."
I'm not either replied Daphne. "Why dont we go over to
the park and sit on a bench to talk for a while.
Nel- "O really!" She wasn't flying for shit.

Finally I forced myself into saying it was late and that
we should all go home. Then I said " Well I guess I'll
see you both if your around next weekend"! Bob looked at
me with a surprised batz stare. I could'nt read what the
hell kind of expression it was. God only knows what she
dished him after I left them. I left them at Columbus
Circle, and walked towards the east side where I took
another cab home. I kept thinking to myself all the
way home that he has my phone number. So the whole affair
is up to him now.

The next night though, which was Sunday, she shows up
at the bar alone. She gives me this demented dish, that
Bob's all mixed up. He does'nt know if he wants girls or
boys. Or wheter he wants a steady boyfreiend, or what the
hell he wants. I did'nt ask her any questions, I was
just letting her dish her ass off. I did'nt even ask wher
he was. I tried to pull the not bothered camp, but I was
really eating my heart out. I have'nt been this bothered
by a number, since I cant remember. I stayed home all
week waiting for the famous phone call. But so far, no
luck. He's the type that can't see himself giging in
either, but I'm almost positive that I left some kind of
an impression on him. I tried every treatment I could
think of. I thought of you laughing when I told him the
shirt he was wearing was very "sharp" and looked so well
on him. Right now I'll just have to sit it out and see
how successful my attempts were. I'll dish you further
on this chapter of " The Life and Loves of Daphne."

As Always -

Daphne

November 20, 1957

Dear Reno,

I had the end of end Saturday nights. I went out despite the fact that my mother and father were up the Bronx at the wake. As usual lately when I go out on the weekend, I pulled the suit and tie scene. And again as usual I went down the 415 bar. I couldn't wait to see if my 5 & 10 beauty would show up again. Well much to my very, very pleasant surprise, he did! . . .

I was thinking of how I used to watch him from across the counter where he worked at the 5 & 10. Of all the times I used to go in there and have coffee or something just for an excuse to see him. And I can't forget the way all the girls in the store used to dish me. When he had asked me recently what I was in there so often, I said I was working in the Roxy show across the street at the time. "Is that why you wore all that makeup?" Yes. If he only knew the way I was dying to talk to him. Of all the times I used to go out even in snowy weather, to see if he was still working there. And of the day I really died when I found out he wasn't anymore, and that I might never see him again. It all seemed like a dream now. The fact that we finally met and were sitting here together in this romantic setting. I used to devise ways of trying to meet him. Or even get to talk to him. I tried once at the store. But very unsuccessfully. It seemed so hopeless! And now this! It was really more than I could have asked for. This was really my week of weekends. I haven't been this bothered by a number, since I can't remember. I stayed home all week waiting for the famous phone call. But so far, no luck. He's the type that can't see himself giving in either, but I'm almost positive that I left some kind of an impression on him. I tried every treatment I could think of. I thought of you laughing when I told him the shirt he was wearing was very "sharp" and looked so well on him. Right now I'll just have to sit it out and see how successful my attempts were.

I'll dish you further on this chapter of "The Life and Loves of Daphne."

As Always,
Love Daphne
... Love and Kisses xxxxxxxxx

I knew if we could find her then we would really have something special. This would prove to be challenging, because these writers used their drag personas when signing their names. Most of them lived with their parents and likely moved several times throughout their lives. There was also the strong possibility they were no longer with us. Sadly, these men would have been in the center of the AIDS crisis in the 1980s.

Roughly two years after the start of my obsession to locate the letter writers, I made another discovery. Tucked between the letters was a discarded envelope from the 1960s, which had somehow been previously overlooked. The name on the back of the empty envelope was Michael Alogna and the distinct handwriting was a perfect match to Daphne's. The return address was from Queens in New York. We looked up the census records of all the Michael Alognas in Queens during the time this letter was mailed. Next, we compared the name to a current census and with help from the internet, broke the list down further to the age we perceived Daphne to be now. Based off this hunch, hours of cold calling began. This proved to be futile and I was nearing the end of the list . . .

The phone rang four times before it was picked up. A man's soft voice on the other end answered. "Hello?"

"Hello," I sang out, hoping this could be the one. "Is this Daphne?" I held my breath. My fingers were crossed so tightly they could snap.

He replied, "Well, that's a name I haven't heard in a while . . ."

Bingo! Daphne was finally found.

It took several months of conversations with Daphne to convince

her to meet in person. When she finally agreed, I flew to New York the next day.

My hand was shaking from excitement as I knocked on the door of Daphne's Upper East Side apartment. After all this time imagining who Daphne was back then and who she might be now, I was about to meet my idol. The door opened slowly to a fragile, elegant, grey-haired Italian man. His delicate voice was so soft as to be inaudible at times; he wore a thin layer of powder on his face with a smudge of liner around the eyes. My Daphne! I immediately felt as though I had known her for years.

Daphne was quite resistant to revisit her long-ago life; she couldn't understand why her stories would be of interest. Deep down there was shame that came with these untold chapters. Daphne was older now and she held onto regret for certain choices she made while navigating New York City in her early years. That chapter in her life was behind her and it would have stayed there too had she not picked up the phone or answered the door. Understandably, her concern was mainly over her fears of what her family would think of her past. Daphne's two lovely nieces, Veronica and Maureen, took special care of her and honestly, she wanted to spare them the sordid details of that time in her life.

On impulse I reached out and held Daphne's hand. Choosing my words carefully I explained the significance of her letters and the impact they have on others. Her writings reveal a rare account of queer life in mid-century America; real LGBTQ+ people persevering against all odds during what was a shameful time. Her letters are educational and provide a lens into a past most people don't know existed. Queer people don't have a clear understanding of their history because it is limited and has been destroyed or shamefully hidden. All that most people know about gay history is Stonewall and AIDS, and we were lucky if someone taught us about Stonewall.

I could feel Daphne squeeze my hand. I looked into her eyes and encouraged her not to be ashamed of her past but to own it! Reminding her the choices we make in life don't define us but shape us, for good or bad. I promised I would share her truth and with everything in my being, I would protect her and continue her legacy beyond her time on this earth. It was a plea; I was not going to leave without Daphne's consent.

Finally, giving my hand another squeeze she stared back at me and with a clever smile whispered, "You have a very symmetrical face, I trust you. Let's do it." I wasn't sure if I was going to laugh or cry!

We managed to contact other drag queens and female illusionists who were in some way connected to my discovery. We sat down with renowned historians who opened more doors through which we found the most notable and lauded cultural anthropologists, authors, and academics in the fields of LGBTQ+ and drag culture. I felt like Dorothy from *The Wizard of Oz* following the yellow brick road and meeting so many wonderful characters along the way who would forever change my life.

It is important to note that I could never have pieced together this history without the support of all these people. This was a communal endeavor for which we all share credit. The scholars were beyond thrilled to see, read, and hold these artefacts of our history. As much of it appeared to be written in code, the historians deconstructed and interpreted the very specific vernacular belonging to this group of young queens. One can feel the urgency of their writing in real time; their elation and frustration captured as if in secret snapshots. These fully candid and confessional narrations allow us in; unfiltered, unedited, and unbothered.

The writings invite us to take a deeper look into a specific time and place that may have been long ago lived but will not soon be forgotten.

CHAPTER TWO

Queer Times and Queer Language

aphne and I took small steps on the wet sidewalk. Holding onto me with her arm hooked through mine, we slowly made our way down Lexington Avenue. Leaves blew across lanes of traffic and danced between the honking cars, as they wrestled with yellow cabs. Dark clouds swallowed the tops of the tallest buildings which disappeared into the mist. A light rain began to fall as we stepped into a piano bar near her apartment. The bar was warm and inviting. There was a mix of antique gold framed paintings of English country scenes and framed newspaper clippings hung at random on top of fading red painted walls. I could feel the history of this joint by looking into the faces of the patrons. This was an older gay establishment with a charming crowd to match.

In the corner, a gray-haired man was plunking away at the keys on the baby grand piano while humming a tune I recognized, "Night and Day" by Cole Porter. Tom, the handsome bartender, greeted us as I was introduced. Daphne had been coming here for years for their unbeatable martinis. I helped her out of her coat and hung it on a hook as we settled into our booth. A few of the older patrons wandered over to the table and chatted with Daphne about her new living arrangements, as she had recently been forced to leave her large apartment of over thirty years to a big developer.

"Out with the old, in with the new," she sighed. "They tore down my old building. I don't like change, but I suppose everything

changes." Rolling her eyes, "Everyone changes." I could sense the
move had taken its toll on her. We sat there for an awkward silent
moment as Tom brought us our drinks.

After taking a sip, Daphne pulled a clear plastic file from out of her
leather satchel; I could see the contents were vintage photographs.
Some of the photos were held together with an old rubber band that
snapped as she separated them and laid them out on the table in
front of us. She handed me a small square photo, date stamped *Sept
1962*. This was the first image I'd ever seen of Daphne in her heyday:
young and beautiful, reclining in a black Knoll butterfly chair. Her
legs were long and smooth, with puffy slippers on her feet; she wore

an oversized black turtleneck, and a curly platinum blonde pixie wig. The vision was finished off with dark red lipstick. Chuckling, she announced with pride she was, "Trying to make the slippers sexy. I was so beautiful then and I had a sensational set of legs!"

I listened astutely, watching Daphne's eyes "light up" as she pulled stories from her memory tied to each incredible image. That afternoon, I became Daphne's passenger as she drove me down memory lane.

The young Daphne in these old photos was exactly how I had been imagining her: soft, demure, confident, and stunningly beautiful. I asked her if she had any letters or photos from Reno. Sadly, she did not. "Those were destroyed long ago," she told me with a sense of regret.

I picked up a glossy 8 × 10 black and white photograph with worn corners that stood out to me. It was a photo of Daphne strutting down a catwalk in a theater wearing an incredible knee-length sheath dress with silver lame ruching and shimmering rhinestone trim detail with perfect puff sleeves in what appeared to be white fur. She was sure to let me know there was a hidden zipper on the left side of the dress which she pulled up from the hem for a big "reveal" of her legs—and they were, indeed, sensational! In the photo the audience was staring up at her on the catwalk from the floor and cheering for her from the balcony above. Daphne was living the moment and it showed on her face as well as the faces of the energetic adoring audience.

Daphne noticed I was astounded by the image! "Billy Norton made me that dress. It was for a ball in Harlem." Looking up to the ceiling she put her hands together as if in prayer. "I love you, Billy—you're an angel!" she announced loudly as though she wanted to shout it up to heaven so Billy would hear her. The table next to us looked over. "She would make you a knockout gown overnight. Such a talent," she continued. "I miss Billy, she was a good friend—a nice Irish boy—never said a mean word to anyone." Then quietly she said, "Taken too soon."

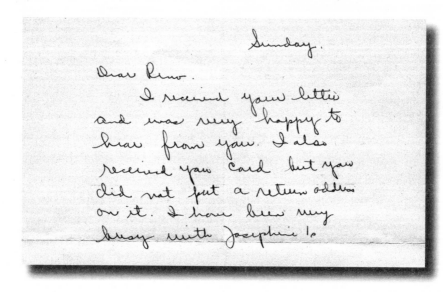

dress. It came out Sensational!!
I could not get to see her
that night but I heard
from Daphne she looked
gorgeous. The drag was suppos
to be on a stick. Josephine
call me yesterday & was very
depressed. After the drag which
was friday night she left
the hotel (new Yorker) where
she dressed & took a cab home.
She pulled the scene on the
hotel bill. She was very
loaded & when leaving the
cab left her suitcase in the
cab. It had her dress, ~~...~~
So just a word of caution Reno,
take good care of yourself & don't
pull ~~...~~ no buts scenes. I don't want
not nothing happing to you. ~~...~~
Take good care - will write soon ~~...~~

Dear Reno

I received your letter and was very happy to hear from you. I also received your card but you did not put a return address on it. I have been very busy with Josephine's dress. It came out sensational!! I could not get to see her that night but I heard from Daphne she looked gorgeous. The drag was suppose to be on a stick ...

Always your friend
Billy

The more time I spent with Daphne, the more I began to understand what dressing up and presenting herself as female meant to her. Playing this role as a female was for the thrill and excitement of pulling off the ultimate taboo; voluntarily giving up male privilege to be perceived as a seductive young woman, even for a night. There was a power in portraying the female illusion and, whether the letter writers knew it or not, their subversion was a living form of resistance and rebellion.

Daphne explained to me, "In those days you had to pass, darling, there were no two ways about it." She continued, "If you couldn't pass, don't do it. Don't do drag—some butch-looking queens would, and they wouldn't get half out the door before they were harassed by the cops. It was dangerous."

I learned there was a stark difference between how these queens were perceived and how they viewed themselves in the 1950s. This was particularly evident in the divisions between what I have termed "Show Queens" and "Street Queens." The Street Queen, a category that included Daphne and the other letter writers, was someone who was not paid to perform or impersonate women. In contrast, Show Queens were professional performers who worked regularly on the nightclub scene. At that time there was no lip synching; it was unheard of. Show Queens were required to have an original "act"—be it singing, dance, striptease or any other gimmick. Some queens were relegated to the chorus while others were booked as headliners and performed for audiences three shows a night, six days a week. The Show Queen preferred to be called a femme mimic or female illusionist.

Show Queens took great care to work and live within the confines of the laws to preserve their professional careers as female illusionists. They were strictly prohibited from appearing in drag anywhere outside of the clubs. As a result, Show Queens and Street Queens rarely mixed. There was a class system, with professional Show Queens at the top of the hierarchical heap and Street Queens relegated to the very bottom. To this day, these older queens shudder at the term "drag queen," which was not used as widely as it is today and was considered derogatory. In the New York of the 1950s, if you were referred to as a drag queen, you were thought of—and called out as—a prostitute.

The gender binary was strictly observed during this time in America and a great deal of public energy was put into enforcing the status quo. As such, the primary goal of the Street Queen was to pass successfully as female to avoid abuse or arrest.

The group of young queens in Reno's letters lived on the edge and would gleefully *mop* (steal) as though it was a game to see who brought in the biggest haul. They risked everything by strutting about the city in their newly mopped attire. They were street smart and savvy. The Boomatzas weren't thinking too far beyond the next gown, ball, or trick. However, as much as they were pushing boundaries, it was clear there was always a threat looming in the back of their minds.

FEBRUARY 13, 1958

Dear Reno,

I've found myself here at work with nothing to do, so I thought it would be a good chance to drop my bummish sister a line. How are you my dear? Is the flame of love still burning brightly in your mascared eyes ? I just hope their not running as a result of a more common outcome. I haven't been over Camille's over the weekend, so I don't know if there were any letters over their from you. The last one I got, revealed the contents of your latest love interest. And interesting indeed it seems. Say how much is the bus fare down to Alexandria? I heard that the weather down around those parts has been quite fatch. I heard they had snow in New Orleans for the first time in twenty years. Your prescence in the vininity must be causing the weather upset. I saw Claudia over the weekend at the 415. She was wearing much the weight-lifter T shirt and Dungarees. Her hair is short and red. She looked bummy. She said the flight scene of herself and Josie has been postponed. So was the drag up here that was supposed to be on for tommorrow night. I'm saving my idea for it for a future scene. I received an invitation to buy tickets for the Artists Equity ball at the Walforf Astoria. They've set the date for the 28th of March. I read earlier in the paper this month that they're trying to get Bridgette Bardot for the queen. Is'nt that a camp? She's such a bum ! I love her. And she'd be such an appropiate one. The title of the ball is Sinerama. Yes with an "S", honey. Isint that too much? I must make the scene. But I'd still rather go as a boy and not in Drag. And besides with Bardott around, who'd stand a chance. I've heard those dishes before, about who they were trying to get for queen of the ball. By the time it gets here though, the queen will most likely be Angela Lansbury. (Then I'll go drag.)

Its four thirty Cindy, and I've got to catch my bus. Listen tommorrow is Valentine's day. Happy lovin !

As Always,

Daphne

February 13, 1958

Dear Reno,

I've found myself here at work with nothing to do, so I thought it would be a good chance to drop my bummish sister a line. How are you my dear? Is the flame of love still burning brightly in you mascared eyes? I just hope their not running as result of a more common outcome. I haven't been over Camille's over the weekend, so I don't know if there were any letters over their from you. The last one I got, revealed the contents of your latest love interest. And interesting indeed it seems. Say how much is the bus fare down to Alexandria? I heard that the weather down around those parts has been quite fatch. I heard they had snow in New Orleans for the first time in twenty years. Your presence in the vicinity must be causing the weather upset. I saw Claudia over the week-end at the 415. She was wearing much the weight-lifter T-shirt and Dungarees. Her hair is short and red. She looked bummy. She said the flight scene of herself and Josie has been postponed. So was the drag up here that was supposed to be on for tomorrow night. I'm saving my idea for it for a future scene. I received an invitation to buy tickets for the Artists Equity ball at the Waldorf Astoria. They've set the date for the 28th of March. I read earlier in the paper this month that they're trying to get Bridgette Bardot for the queen. Is'nt that a camp? She's such a bum! I love her. And she's be such an appropriate one. The title of the ball is Sinerama. Yes with an "S" honey. Isn't that too much? I must make the scene. But I'd still rather go as a boy and not in Drag. And besides with Bardot around, who'd stand a chance. I've heard those dishes before, about who they were trying to get for queen of the ball. By the time it gets here though, the queen will most likely be Angela Lansbury. (Then I'll go drag.)

As Always, Daphne

Daphne couldn't get dressed at home, so the solution was the "trick room". She and her friends would rent a small furnished room by the month, for about seventy-five dollars, in a run-down tenement building in the middle of Times Square, which during the 1950s was thought of as a seedy part of New York. They shared the trick room with a like-minded group, three female prostitutes known as the Glamazons. These gorgeous cis women were tall and curvaceous, with added height from their overprocessed and teased beehive hairdos. The trick room was primarily used as a crash pad and safe space to get ready for what the night had in store. It was also the place to stash anything the queens mopped: clothes, wigs, jewelry and whatever their arms could carry. As you might have guessed, the trick room lived up to its name; it was also a place to entertain paying customers, because sex work was a quick and easy way to make much-needed cash.

One time, Fleet Week had arrived, and the city was buzzing with new trade. The navy had come to town! The Boomatzas and the Glamazons took this week very seriously, because these girls were about to take on the troops. The trick room was in full swing with Daphne and three Glams. All the girls, in various states of dress, readied themselves as they navigated around each other in the crowded room. Applying makeup on top of makeup, these girls competed for that extra "naughty" look.

Daphne, feeling satisfied with her makeup, sat down on a stool while one of the Glams pinned two bouncy dark brown wigs on top of her head, whipping it all into a tousled updo. It was a bit much for Daphne normally, but it was perfect for tonight. After all, she had to consider her audience. More than the cash, Daphne was looking forward to the thrill of meeting a handsome sailor; there was something about a man in a uniform that made her bite her bottom lip. Adjusting herself in the mirror she felt beautiful in a tight, teal blue knee-length dress she borrowed from Josephine. The black stilettos she mopped from Bloomingdale's completed the look.

New York was sweating through a heat wave and the warm nights brought out the masses. 42nd Street was bustling with activity. Sailors littered every street corner, wreaking havoc on any girl in earshot by cat calling, whistling and professing their undying love, as they passed on the sidewalk.

Daphne and the Glams met up with her friends and the scene was on! The "girl pack" prowled 42nd Street, ducking in and out of bars teeming with rowdy sailors aiming to make the most of their leave. Fights broke out at random, and some sailor had a bottle smashed over his head, another caught a right cut to the jaw. Witnessing this, Daphne decided humidity and booze were a bad combination for boys who have been cooped up together on a ship for months at a time. The night wore on and one by one each girl disappeared from the group and into the crowd after negotiating with a sailor.

Now Daphne was seated on the edge of the bed in the trick room. Through the wall she heard a girl laying into a john for stiffing her ten bucks. Daphne turned up the radio to drown out the commotion. Turning her attention back to the room, she watched one of the Glams lift a uniform shirt over the head of the tall, inebriated sailor the two had found wandering the sidewalk in front of their building. Daphne surveyed his solid frame. He was good looking bum. *He'll do*, she thought to herself. The shirtless sailor flung himself onto the bed, holding on to a bottle of whiskey, contemplating his next move with each of the two girls.

The Glam took the initiative: lifting her skirt, she climbed on top of the young man, straddling him. After some time, Daphne, not being able to contain her own excitement, reached over and put her hand gently on the sailor's thigh. Slowly he looked over at Daphne and without words, he pushed the Glamazon off him with enough force she lost her balance and rolled onto the floor. He abruptly swung his legs off the bed, stood up and opened the door to the hall.

"Get out!" he demanded. Daphne stood up from the bed. "Not you," he tossed a look to the girl on the floor, "her." Slowly the Glam picked herself up off the floor, pulled her skirt down and walked to the door. Turning back to Daphne she gave a thumbs up.

Daphne was alone with the sailor. He stepped toward her and stood silently in front of her, staring at her as if analyzing her. Daphne's heart was beating fast and for a quick moment she felt unsure of his motives. Her fear was fleeting as he leaned down and kissed her. Daphne could taste the whiskey on his breath. He ran his hand down her back while kissing her neck. She closed her eyes, throwing her head back while reaching down placing her hand on his groin. She smiled, pleased with herself, discovering she was able to accomplish what the Glam couldn't. Then, looking past Daphne, out of nowhere he asked, "Can I try on that grass skirt?"

Surprised by the request, Daphne's eyes scanned the room and there it was—the grass skirt hanging on a hook.

"Of course, honey!" She was more than happy to oblige . . .

"I helped him out of his civvies so fast!" Daphne could barely contain her excitement while recounting this story. She didn't need to tell me what happened next, as I already knew. But she was sure to let me know, "It was the first time I enjoyed holding a twenty-dollar bill!" she winked.

Daphne was equally thrilled she had triumphed over a beautiful biological woman! She also informed me the Boomatzas and the Glamazons never competed when it came to trade, as they all knew too well they weren't being sought after for the same thing.

Two martinis in, and I couldn't have been happier as I sat in the booth listening to Daphne share her life stories with me, pointing out people and faces in the photos she'd carried with her to the piano bar that afternoon. She opened up to me and the stories spilled out of her in vivid detail. It was evident in these letters Daphne was a storyteller, and this characteristic was no less pronounced in person. It occurred to me, she'd locked away these memories and hadn't recalled them in a very long time. That afternoon, it was as though her memories took on a life of their own, as though they wanted to be told and heard at least one more time.

Since most of the letter writers lived with their parents, they would sign with their drag name for fear that a family member, landlord or neighbor would open the envelope and read what was inside. If evidence of homosexuality or wearing drag was discovered, they risked being kicked out of their homes, fired from their jobs, being marked as a communist and excommunicated from society. Names were written up in the papers for unlawful activity and, in many cases, deviants faced jail time. The lengths a family member would go to to keep such shameful secrets from other people meant any written legacy was most likely hidden, destroyed, and long forgotten. This is one example as to why reliable documentation about drag culture prior to the 1990s is largely non-existent.

> Dear Reno;   November 2, 1957
> Hope everything is alright with you. Well, as I am writing this letter, I am burning mad. I'll dish the scene, hope you understand it.
> First, I'll start off with the fact that Charlie's Phone has been disconnected for about a week + a half. Second, almost all week, Charlie has been telling me about this party this queen is giving in the Bronx but didn't know if it was Friday or Saturday night. I told her to call me Friday night if the party was on, because I'd rather go to the party than the drag show, well I left my [?] at about 9, and no call. Today Saturday I ran into Veto on the ave. She told me the scene. There was a party at Al's house, Charlie come in drag, also that queen Ray, that number I told you about from Gimbels. Charlie was there with his friends, I saw red, but didn't let on to Veto that I was bothered. Reno! now understand about the Phone, OK, I could not get in touch with her, how come she didn't call me. I know Chickie was with her and she could have called from the corner. Now I am waiting to run into the big drag queen, to see what her excuse is as if I don't know already, she'll say uh

but you were going to the drag, so I
didn't bother calling, Well she could
save all her excuses, because I am going
to let her have it, she pulled her
last scene on this Jerk. Also how
convenient not having me at the party
so she could carry on anyway she wanted
and wear anything like your black dress.

Yes, this is the queen who you favor
over me, in her glory while you are
away, wearing her famous sweater inside
out, blue mascara, waving her hands
out of cors at trade, and then saying
trade cracks over her,

I know you think I act like you,
and I tried to stop, but this is nothing
to the way fat girl acts, who ae also
become an authority, on hair, trade
etc, she is also starting to call me leek
lady, and I don't like it, I know she
has a girlish face, and is better looking
than me, but she would nearer (con't)
have the nerve I have to cruise trade.

I only hope when you come back
you look more gorgeous than ever,
to show her up, and all these other
demented fags up around here.

Well, I went to pick Daphne up
Friday night, and from there we went to
Lennies, Hideaway in the Village, for a
few drinks, about 11:30 we left to go
to the drag, on the way we passed Everards
and saw a blonde beauty going in,
we almost were going to go in ourselfs but
went to the drag instead,

I repeat she did it again she looked

great, she didn't crap the place up as
much as in Jersey, but she mopped, she
had on a gold dress with red hair,
Pretty boy Johnnie looked good too.
I met, Frankie, Gigi and Georgie
there, there was very little trade and
many queens in costumes, it was over early
and Daphne, steve and this queen in
drag and myself went to this party in the
Village, it was very nelsts, more queens
in costumes, we left, had coffee and
I drove Daphne home I got home about 5 ours

I guess I'll just hang out in Yonkers
or go downtown from now on, and let
the star and her crowd take over the
diner scene, not that there mopping going
on, but at least it was a place to hang out

Getting back to that party at als house
Veta said Charlie looked gay, she had
on your black wig, and that Ray looked
a mess and had some nerve going in
drag she's as fat as a cow,

I also broke down and called Nick
and gave her your address, so I guess
you'll be hearing from her soon

Sorry I have to write all this
while you are so far away, but I had
to get it out of my system,

Please write and let me know
what you think of all this, I'll be
waiting for your next letter, write soon,

Your Friend
Joe

November 2, 1957

Dear Reno,

Hope everything is allright with you. Well, as I am writing this letter, I am burning mad. I'll dish the scene, hope you understand it.

First I'll start off with the fact that Charlie's phone has been disconnected for about a week and a half. Second, almost all week, Charlie has been telling me about this party this queen is giving in the Bronx but didn't know if it was Friday or Saturday night. I told her to call me friday night if the party was on, because I'd rather I left my house at about 9, and no call. Today Saturday, I ran into Veto on the Ave she told me the scene. There was a party at Al's house, Charlie came in drag, also that queen Raj, that number I told you about from Gimbels. Charlie was there with his friends, I saw red, but didn't let on to Veto that I was bothered. Reno! You understand about the phone, O.K. I could not get in touch with her. How come she didn't call me I know Chickie was with her and she could have called from the corner. Now I am waiting to run into the big drag queen, to see what her excuse is as if I don't know already, she'll say oh but you were going to the drag, so I didn't bother calling. Well she could save all her excuses, because I am going to let her have it, she pulled her last scene on this Jerk. Also how convenient not having me at the party so she could carry on anyway she wanted. Yes, this is the queen you favor over me, in her glam while you are away, wearing her famous sweater inside out, blue mascara, waving her hands out of cars at trade, and then saying trade cracks over her.

I know you think I act like you and I tried to stop, but this is nothing to the way fat girl acts, who has also become an authority, on hair, trade, etc. She is also starting to call me "Beak Lady', and I don't like it. I know she has a girlish face and is better looking than me, but she would never have the nerve I have, to cruise trade.

I only hope when you come back you look more gorgeous

than ever, to show her up, and all these other demented fags up around her.

Well, I went to pick Daphne up Friday night, and from there we went to Lonnie's Hideaway in the Village, for a few drinks, about 11:30 we left to go to the drag. On the way we passed Everard's and saw a blonde beauty going in, we almost were going to go in ourselves but went to the drag instead.

Josephine did it again she looked great, she didn't crack the place up as much as in Jersey, but she mopped she had on a gold dress with red hair. Pretty boy Johnnie looked good too. I met Frankie, GiGi, and Georgie there. There was very little trade and many queen[s] in costumes, it was over early and Daphne, Steve, and this queen in drag and myself went to this party in the Village. It was very nexted, more queens in costumes. We left, had coffee and I drove Daphne home. I got home about 5.

I guess I'll just hang out in Yonkers or go downtown from now on and let the star and her crowd take over the diner scene, not that there's mopping going on, but at least it was a place to hang out.

Getting back to the party at Al's house, Veto said Charlie looked gay and that Raj looked a mess and had some nerve going in drag she's as fat as a cow.

Sorry I have to write all this while you are so far away, but I had to get it out of my system.

Please write and let me know what you think of all this. I'll be waiting for your next letter, write soon.

Your Friend, Joe

CHAPTER THREE

Show Queens

Although it was illegal to be on the street in drag, Show Queens were protected while performing on stage through cabaret licenses. To remain employed, the male performers were required to enter and exit the clubs in male attire, and the female waiters entered and exited in a dress or skirt; otherwise, the establishment could be shut down due to the prohibitive laws of the time.

Club owners found ways to profit from the gay community at the same time as protecting them. There was an unspoken gay tax to keep the spaces running and the clientele safe. Who did this better than anyone, utilising secret, lucrative relationships with police and government? The mafia. Most of the clubs in New York were mob owned and operated, and there was a lot of money to be made from the homosexual community. Although the mafia wasn't a strong supporter of the gay community outwardly, they were happy to benefit from the pink dollar. One could argue, if it wasn't for the mafia there would be no drag queens and certainly there would have been no place for gay culture to have persevered in the 1950s.

These clubs were considered tourist destinations and the audiences consisted of predominantly straight couples on a date or married couples out for a night of taboo, risqué entertainment. This was an opportunity for "regular society" to see gay people parading around in female attire. Understandably, this was a draw for heterosexuals because it was rare for them to even know an openly queer person, and most had never seen a female impersonator. It was an exhibition, a rarity—like seeing an albino tiger at the zoo. Undeniably, the audience was enthralled by the exotic, titillating spectacle they would not soon forget.

While a few exclusive female illusionist nightclubs existed, such as the Moroccan Village and The Jewel Box Revue; the most celebrated and successful of these establishments was the 82 Club located on East 4th Street.

The 82 Club had an unassuming façade that provided no clue as to what lay beneath. To enter, one descended a steep staircase to a smoky basement. Once inside, customers were greeted by the hostess, a diminutive woman whose overly painted black-ringed eyes never missed a trick. This was Anna "the Bun" Genovese, proprietor and wife to Vito, one of the most infamous mob bosses in the

country, and head of the notorious Genovese crime family. What Anna lacked in physical stature—not clearing five feet in heels—she more than made up for in presence. In addition to her signature eyeliner, her black hair was pulled back severely and piled high on top of her head for added height. The Show Queens called her "The Bun" and she was a serious, no-nonsense businesswoman, seen as an enigma, but generous and protective of her performers.

Upon taking their seats at a white linen clothed table among the palms in glossy white plastic pots and tropical decor, customers' drink orders would be taken by a tuxedoed waiter, perhaps by the name of Butch. One of the gimmicks of the club was the waiters were all women in drag king finery to offset the Show Queens on stage. Extremely avant-garde for the time! Along with the everyday patrons there was also a rotating roster of celebrity clientele. On any given night, a guest might have the added pleasure of seeing Elizabeth Taylor and Richard Burton, Jack and Jackie Kennedy, or Judy Garland.

As the house lights dimmed, casting the audience in darkness, colored lights slowly began to flood the stage. The fifteen-piece orchestra struck up with gusto for the entrance of Ty Bennett, the master of ceremonies extraordinaire, a seasoned headliner in full camp glamor drag. She delighted the audience with her bawdy comic genius, setting the tone for the evening. Laughter rang through the audience as the show began to unfold and thirty-five cast members waited in the wings.

An observant customer might notice the world-renowned surrealist and frequent patron, Salvador Dali, sitting in a high-backed booth sketching on a cocktail napkin before directing a waiter to deliver it backstage on a silver tray. The sketch, like hundreds before it over the years, was intended for the one performer who inspired Dali most: headliner Baby Ella-Funt. With a roll of her double lashed eyes and a grunt, she would invariably crumple up the priceless drawing and toss it into the trash. Clearly, she either wasn't aware of the famous Dali or just didn't care. Backstage,

Baby Ella-Funt *takes it off !!!*

Terry "Teri" Noel, the beautiful blonde chorus girl with exquisite features and a body to match, would be going over a new combination in her head while counting under her breath, *5-6-7-8* . . . While the new girl from Canada, Robin Tyler, aka Stacy Morgan, sat on a folding chair nearby with both hands firmly trying to steady her shaking knees before she made her American debut as a drag headliner.

Robin created an act in which she sang "Somewhere Over the Rainbow" as Judy Garland. But gender performativity was subverted yet further, as the audience didn't know that the Canadian born twenty-year-old was a woman pretending

TERI NOEL

to be man pretending to be a woman. Genius! It should be noted that she was the only cisgender woman to have her own act at the club. As a self-titled butch dyke, Robin had no idea how to walk in a heel let alone glue on an eyelash. Taking pity on the fledgling entertainer, the more experienced illusionists took Robin under their feathered wings and showed her the sequined ropes.

Prior to the 82 Club, Robin survived the conservative times by "passing" as a young boy in the streets of Greenwich Village. Because of her youthful appearance and 5' 2" athletic frame, people assumed she was a fourteen-year-old boy running odd jobs to make a buck, and as a result she wasn't harassed. But eventually that illusory bubble burst.

Robin and her friends were attending a drag ball in late October, close to Halloween. There among the hundreds of other attendees stood Robin in her casual shirt and pants. Without warning the doors burst open, and cops spilled through the entrance with whistles blowing. Thinking it an unpermitted event, they raided the ball, arresting a number of queens. When Robin challenged the police they grabbed her as well, assuming she was a boy, and pushed her into the back of a police wagon.

Sent to a holding cell with the queens, Robin was given her one phone call. Naturally resourceful, she took full advantage of this opportunity. Since attorneys would not represent a queer person in those days, she made contact with the *New York Post*, telling the reporter what had just happened to her and the others which resulted in the article "Cops Grab 44 Men and a Real Girl in Slacks."

There were a few other exceptions in which club owners were willing to bend their otherwise iron-clad rules. Terry Noel, another of the 82 Club's Show Queens, was one of them. Terry was part of the chorus line and, like many before her, found community in NYC that she sorely lacked in her small hometown. Terry felt most like her authentic self while presenting as a woman, not in the male form she had been assigned since birth, an assignment that never fit no matter how she tried to align her inner and outer self. After a few years working at the 82 Club and learning more about her own gender identity, Terry realized that she was living with such a seemingly irreconcilable conflict and was in fact transgender. In the 1950s the term used was transsexual, as transgender hadn't yet been coined. At that time there was only one known American who had undergone gender reassignment through hormone therapy and surgery in Denmark: Christine Jorgensen. There was little, if any, reliable information for anyone questioning their gender identity or who identified as transsexual. Even more challenging was the task of locating a legitimate, knowledgeable doctor to oversee medical transitions.

Terry, however, was fortunate enough to find tremendous support in a most unlikely ally: Anna Genovese, the hostess and owner of the 82 Club. Terry and Anna had always gotten along very well, and when Anna learned of Terry's truth, she insisted on helping her. Anna arranged for Terry to see her personal doctor in Brooklyn, who not only prescribed and administered Terry's hormone therapy, but never charged her a cent. It was all taken care of by Anna. As time went by and Terry continued in her transition and underwent her first of two gender reassignment surgeries in Chicago.

Upon her return to New York, Terry was concerned with how she would support herself financially while acclimating to her new life. Once again, Anna came to Terry's rescue. Even though one of the steadfast rules was that Show Queens were male to female illusionists, Anna was more than willing to make an exception in Terry's case. No one in the cast knew of Terry's surgery and Anna made sure it remained that way.

But for every story of staunch sisterhood and community, there was drama between the performers, too. The spectre of "The Ripper" haunted the dressing room at the 82 Club. The Ripper was an unidentified queen who habitually cut other performers' sequined and tailored costumes to shreds, in an effort to squash the competition or enact revenge for a previous slight. It was not uncommon to hear an unsuspecting queen screeching from the dressing room after discovering some other vicious queen had crushed glass into a fine dust and mixed it in to the targeted victim's face powder.

One high point of the evening was a striptease performance of Salome's "Dance of the Seven Veils." The star of the spectacle was Cuban-born Adrian, a female illusionist who was part of the "Ladies in Hades" revue and embodied the role of the eponymous heroine. Adrian was a dancer. Her petite frame was suggestively covered in flowing, colored scarves and jewelry. Adrian's gamine stare seduced the audience into submission as her body writhed and convulsed hypnotically, stripping layers of clothing away. The dance built to a crescendo when Adrian revealed and caressed the severed head of John the Baptist, by which point the din of the audience, beating their table knocker batons, drowned out the orchestra. *Brava!* Adrian was a star performer at the 82 and her act was lauded as a "Must see!" Audiences and performers came from all over to experience it.

As much as people enjoyed the show witnessing extraordinary talent, there was also an undercurrent of homophobia that couldn't be denied. Performers were encouraged to walk through the crowd during sets and mingle with the guests. Often men, and occasionally women, had a visceral reaction to a queen as she approached their table. Stigma was in the air. It was fine when the performers were entertaining from the stage, but up close and personal, that was a different feeling.

The dichotomy of female impersonation being revered on the stage and reviled on the street is not lost here. These nightclubs were a ritualised space. Audiences knew what the illusion was, which made it safe. Street Queens, on the flipside, were enacting a form of rebellion any time they stepped out in full drag. There wasn't an alternative to passing if a queen wanted to avoid abuse on the street unless they could walk down the sidewalk and blend into their surroundings.

CHAPTER FOUR

Street Queens

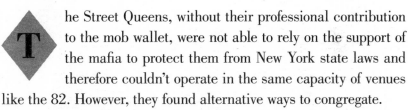

The Street Queens, without their professional contribution to the mob wallet, were not able to rely on the support of the mafia to protect them from New York state laws and therefore couldn't operate in the same capacity of venues like the 82. However, they found alternative ways to congregate.

The letter writers would frequent known gay-friendly bars like the Cork Club and Bon Soir wearing "boy" clothes, with a subtle touch of mascara or lip gloss as a signal. That alone could get them in trouble. It was a rule not to come in drag, because if the bar was found out to be openly catering to drag queens, they would risk losing their liquor permit and be shut down. A cluster of bars along Third Avenue in the midtown area, primarily catering to gay patrons, was known as "the bird circuit." With names like The Swan, The Blue Parrot, and The Golden Pheasant, they were coded as safe places to gather, though certainly not immune from police raids. When things got too hot with the clubs being raided, they would take their show on the road to suburbs outside the city.

from letter dated Sept. 11, 1957

Dear Reno

The cops have practically moved into the diner, the scene is off for hanging out there.

Joe

Through the gay network on the streets, Sreet Queens found other public spaces and would meet discreetly without fear of being raided. On most days at 4 p.m. the boys would dress in suit and tie and descend onto the Waldorf Astoria as it was a gathering place for "tea." The queens would sit in the light of day and dish about the night before, a trick and each other.

February 2, 1958

Dear Reno

... we stopped at the Waldorf, it was packed. Josephine, Daphne and some other queens from Brooklyn were there, many fights broke out the cops came and almost the whole place cleaned out, and I heard the place is going to get raided so that's the end of that scene.

—Joe

But places that allowed queer people to be authentically themselves, without fear of recrimination, were few and far between. Either they were the entertainment, or they were in danger, and navigating these spaces in public life was fraught with peril. However, it was only in these spaces that the letter writers were able to meet one another and form the close friendships that are revealed in the letters and came to define their lives at this time.

Roberto Perez came to America from Puerto Rico with his family when he was barely a teenager. His parents uprooted the family and settled in New York City in search of the American Dream. Roberto's Spanish father was a proud man who didn't have a clear understanding of his misunderstood son as he grew into a teenager. Roberto was spending less time at home and his father found his teenage son harder to control. Mr. Perez's disappointment was compounded when it was learned his son began working part-time as a hairdresser's assistant in Chelsea.

Roberto was off to his own devices as he spread his wings and stepped out into the world. With this new freedom he decided the city was his playground. And why not? New York City was exciting and alive in the 1950s! He much preferred it to where he'd grown up as a boy in San Juan. Here in America, Roberto's heart beat to the rhythm of the streets, which he found intoxicating. Always daring, he had the name "Josephine" tattooed onto his back, behind the right shoulder in cursive script as an homage to his teenage obsession, the first international black superstar, Josephine Baker. Roberto adopted the name of his idol to fit his own drag persona and the vivacious Josephine was born! Her signature look was a black wig with blunt cut baby bangs. The long strands of hair pulled back tight into a switch, that hung down to her waist. Quick-witted Josephine wore her new armor like a second skin and could dissect a cynic with the lash of her tongue. She was both a lover and a fighter.

Dear Reno:

nov. 19 - 1957

Oh! last nite I was coming home in the rain & this kid followed me with an umbrella & a suitcase so the rain was coming down very heave and I heard the footsteps behind me so I stopped & dished & got under the umbrella with him (not bothered) & stared to dish well anyway hes my ~~other~~ neighbor & hes in the play (My Fair Lady) isnt that a flipp! what an adorable face he has & a freeky piece of meat, well he gave me the end blow job & I jerked him off & caught the load it was so tremendous & carried on in my hallway so we coulnt do too much such is rimming & banging but the scene is on I know it! hes a little gay (Ha Ha) so I have to go to his place Friday I think It could be a steady bang or something Ill work something out with him Im sure. hes no beauty & wears glasses but the face & body are very turnish gorgeus lips.

well listen they closed Stonwood for good! I still paint of course silly - & my brows are grown but cleverly cleaned & penciled, Georgie & Tony L are the only Batz ones left. & there one the kick but some how they cant kick the habit (the tweezers).

well phil Black is soon and Im not making it for the first time in dragg. theres no scene for me I gave up. Im disgusted with drag really! that last one did the trick. fuck that Ratzile neil Bell. maybe for the future Waldorf or something gay Ill go I sold the red wig to Sally Blane & the gold dress is flying too. so listen it all in "vain".

Love Jo Baker

November 19, 1957

Dear Reno

Oh! Last nite I was coming home in the rain and this kid followed me with an umbrella + a suitcase so the rain was coming down very heavy and I heard the footsteps behind me so I stopped + dished + got under the umbrella with him (not bothered) + started to dish well anyway he's my neighbor + he's in the play (My Fair Lady) isn't that a flipp! What an adorable face he has + a freaky piece of meat, well he gave me the end blow job + I jerked him off + caught the load it was so tremendous and carried on in my hallway so we couldn't do too much such as rimming+ banging but the scene is on I know it! He's a little gay (Ha Ha) so I have to go to his place Friday. I think it could be a steady bang or something. I'll work something out with him I'm sure. He is a beauty and wears glasses but the face + body are very bummish gorgeous lips.

love, Jo Baker

Josephine used her drag as a lure. She was able to fool most straight or questioning men into giving up their hard-earned cash for a stolen moment of satisfaction. She was the life of the party and loved being the center of attention, in or out of drag.

Unfortunately, word of Josephine's illicit behavior traveled through the tight-knit Puerto Rican neighborhoods, and it was only a matter of time before Mr. Perez would have to confront his son, who still lived at home. His father's abashment was equally shared with his wife, who while rooting around Josephine's bedroom discovered a stash of makeup Josephine had stolen with her new friend, Claudio Diaz.

Josephine and Claudio's chance meeting happened one night out at the Cork Club. Josephine was standing in front of one of the four booths that lined the back wall in full drag attire. Claudio was brought to the club that night by a beautiful boy he had a secret crush on from his neighborhood, by the name of Fayo. The bar was filled that evening and despite being with his crush, Claudio couldn't take his eyes off the beautiful young woman standing nearly six feet tall, smoking a long pink cigarette which, not by coincidence, coordinated with her off-the-shoulder pink taffeta sheath dress that stopped at the knees and had a matching grosgrain ribbon belt attached under the bust.

When Josephine turned and looked in Claudio's direction, they locked eyes. Josephine's infectious smile and warmth was unlike anything he had ever felt. They became instant friends and to Claudio's surprise, not one person could have mattered more from that moment on.

The youngest of the queens, Claudio was also Puerto Rican. He was born in New York in the 1940s and the child of an unwed sixteen-year-old. This young Catholic girl was considered unfit to raise her son due to her immaturity and issues with alcohol. Branded a whore, she was kicked out of her parents' home soon after Claudio was born. His traditional Catholic grandfather couldn't bear having his daughter around to remind him of his own shortcomings in rearing such an abomination, and he was determined not to repeat the past with this new baby.

His grandmother wanted nothing to with Claudio. Her resentment toward him only grew after his grandfather "Pops" passed away at an

early age. Suddenly she was forced to raise this unwanted child on her own. Her hostility toward Claudio resulted in abuse.

From his earliest memories, Claudio felt unworthy of love. He received no affection from his grandmother or his biological mother, who was often drunk when he was able to see her. He became the whipping boy and was punished just for being alive. Called a freak at home and at school, young Claudio Diaz had no sense of security or safety. It was only a matter of time before the mental and physical abuse took hold of his psyche and he began to believe he was worthless.

Josephine was already a fixture in the underground gay clubs. She introduced Claudio to a more glamorous, open world, far from his home, and it wasn't long before the best friends became drag sisters, often seen together at the Cork Club. After all, it was an easy step for Claudio to become "Claudia." This popular pair were allowed to frequent certain underground gay clubs in drag because they could easily blend in as real women. If the bar was raided, they would exit the same way they came in, through the front door. They were as feminine as one could be, to the envy of some of the other queens as they would easily pass as authentic girls on the streets.

As beautiful as they were, Josephine and her counterpart Claudia had something of a bad reputation. Young, glamorous and amorous they may have been, they also liked to take other people's things. They stole everything—your heart and your wallet! It was no surprise trouble seemed to follow them.

This pair was often spotted roaming the streets in the village and Harold Square in full drag dodging police and vice who were patrolling with the end goal of arresting degenerates and perverts masquerading as female. There was challenge in this, but there were even bigger, more alluring challenges to take on in a city as bustling and cosmopolitan as New York.

High society events and balls were commonplace for heterosexual patrons in New York City during the 1950s and something took place nearly every weekend somewhere in the city. It was a game for Daphne and Josephine to insert themselves into straight society, if only to see what they could get away with.

Daphne and Josephine decided to go in full head to toe drag and crash a very respectable dance at the Plaza Hotel. They had no trouble passing as women or gaining entrance. Their dance cards began to fill as they carried on through the event, powdering their noses in the Women's Lounge, being offered champagne and hors d'oeuvres. They rested their satin gloved hands on the shoulders of tall, handsome, tuxedoed men as they were effortlessly swept around the grand ballroom in beautiful gowns that had been created by Billy Baker. They kept their words to a minimum as not to give any hint of their masquerade.

Josephine and Daphne felt like debutantes in New York society and were getting the royal treatment. However, rumors began to circulate through the ballroom that a couple of "men wearing dresses" had infiltrated the dance. When the unsuspecting gentleman

Daphne was dancing with leaned down and told her there might be some female impersonators there, her eyes widened as her soul left body. With a nervous giggle, she graciously thanked him for the dance, immediately found Josephine, in the arms of a handsome stranger, and got out at the stroke of midnight without being clocked.

Not one, but two Cinderfellas descended quickly down the wide stairs and ran out of the Plaza Hotel, laughing all the way back to the trick room!

CHAPTER FIVE

Sex and Sex Work

he quest for sex is a recurring theme in the letters. They were having sex. A lot of sex. The writers don't go into immense detail regarding the type of sex they are having unless it is in code.

Sex was not a topic people discussed openly in the 1950s. Heterosexual sex between a man and a woman was "normal," but only acceptable as husband and wife and relegated for procreation. The missionary position was acceptable for heterosexuals and sexual exploration other than this was taboo. Of course, any action that was performed between same-sex couples was illegal. The letters establish that some writers took more chances than others, but generally the sexual acts referenced consisted of oral satisfaction and consensual mutual masturbation.

Where the writers had sex depended on the type of sexual behavior they engaged in. It is also important to consider their ages and what kind of source material was available for them to self-educate as to how to perform certain sex acts. Because of age, home circumstances and the illegal nature of the liaisons, I assume the act was quick and less imaginative when compared to the evolution of today's standards. Oral sex and masturbation could be achieved readily out and about New York City, making it convenient and appealing.

According to the letters, the queens were having sex wherever they could—often they were going to a tea room or the "pink" tea room at a bar or a club. (What they are referring to is sexual activity in a men's or women's restroom.) Everard's is referenced (a bath house), Joe's car doubled as a place to entertain—which came in handy—and of course, there was the famous trick room. Sometimes there would be several people in the trick room at the same time, but there isn't evidence that it was anything more than oral in these situations.

September 11, 1957

Dear Reno:

Hope everything is all right with you. Some funny things have been happening here ...

I mopped on this blonde beauty Erick, from my neighborhood the other night, I've had him a few times before, but never alone, this time I did and had the end scene I S–HIS–A, he has the end buns, if I ever get him alone again I'll try the scene.

I never told any of you but I was nuts about this kid for a long time, and would just love to mop on him ever night (Don't Laugh) . . .

if you need anything let me know.

By the way how are your eyebrows:

HA HA HA

"Yours until I give up trade"

Love Joe

P.S. I S-His-A means: (I sucked his ass)

Sexual activity takes place in real time, and the writer's own accounts spelled out the types of activities taking place. For example, when Joe writes Reno informing him he did an "S-HIS-S scene" you can almost feel his internal giddiness. This was something he couldn't keep to himself and he breaks the "gay letter code" by writing the meaning: "Suck his ass." This was a big deal for Joe! So big he had to share it with his best friend.

So I went to the doctors and he gave medicine for my cold

Well things are pretty much the same, I still am not dishing the a vera much and Mascon and Sal haven't come to terms as yet so things are pretty much the same as when you left.

We are still mopping o. mamma and a lot of chicken from the neighborhood as I have a lot of young kids from the neighborhood strickly doing them for trade no scenes on buses.

Well I am not working as I got laid off last weds.

Please excuse my handwriting but I am very bragged and my handwriting isn't steady. take care
Regards from all Gigi

September 23

Dear Reno—

I am sorry I didn't write sooner but I haven't been feeling too well. I went to the hospital today and I have to go to the Med Clinic. I think I have hemorrhoids and it is killing what pain. I had got banged last Friday 3 times in one night and then again 2 days later and I think it was too much. Then I was sick with a terrible throat cold and dizzy spells. So I went to the doctors and he gave me medicine for my cold.

Gigi

GiGi was a good girl. She may not have been the prettiest in drag, when compared to the other queens, but she did alright out on the streets when it came to cruising and picking up trade. She knew she had to work a little harder competing for the boys. When it came to cruising, GiGi found she did much better on her own when she wasn't in the shadow of the Boomatzas. Her sense of humor was her secret weapon, and she used it, knowing if all else fails—be funny. She had it down, too: GiGi made fun of herself first, making it impossible for anyone to make a joke at her expense, or a slight behind her back. She swept up after herself and kept a clean sidewalk.

New Jersey was her playground, and she pulled many scenes in and out of drag. Picking up trade in her own neighborhood was easy enough because GiGi had no inhibitions when it came to sex, she would do it anywhere in public: on buses, in the trains—it didn't matter who it was with as long as she was getting something out of it. Being friendly, she would meet someone new and right away consider them a friend. GiGi was a pleaser and because of this she had a hard time saying no.

Being the friendly, approachable Boomatza had its disadvantages. GiGi often put herself in uncomfortable situations when it came to sex and was forcibly taken advantage of by regular trade and others from the neighborhood. GiGi experienced medical issues from repeated exposure to intercourse. From her accounts, I can assume the act wasn't being properly executed. GiGi and Charlie aside, I don't believe the writers were experiencing intercourse regularly. One thing is clear, they were experiencing sexual activity with multiple partners.

Cruising was the foundation of gay male life in the 1950s. This act happened in public spaces and was perhaps the most spontaneous and sure-fire way to meet someone. Cruising would happen on the streets, parks, public bathrooms, and the docks to name a but few venues; cruising could happen anywhere two people could exchange an unspoken communication. "Signaling" was a silent gesture and as important as the act of cruising—these actions went hand in hand, the most obvious signs being a lingering stare, a subtle nod or shift in one's body language. Signals could also be wearing a hint of makeup or a particular article of clothing. A drag queen was a walking signal.

Dear Reno:

I hope everything is OK with you. I am fine and hope you are to. Well I spent a very busy week out almost every night for a change much cruising, my new scenes are in the Bronx now. I cruised a beauty on Boston Road the other night. I picked him up and he lived across the Bridge he said he had to be home early and would meet me 8:30 Friday night well as my luck goes, he didn't shine. "oh well" So you know it's been about two weeks since I mopped, I

My Mother leaves for Florida tomorrow so I'll have to do much cooking and cleaning while she's away, and how are

You making out with your new lover, OK I hope, it must be a gay scene.

And our dear girl Charlie is back in the swing of things again, back at the Diner and her usual routine I guess. Its now going on a Month since Ive been hanging out at that Diner and I don't miss it a bit.

All the queens got the Bon-ray at the Strand in Yonkers so thats the end of that place.

Love Joe.

from letter dated February 2, 1958

Dear Reno:

I hope everything is OK with you, I am fine and hope you are to. Well I spent a very busy week out almost every night for a change much cruising, my new scenes are in the Bronx now, I cruised a beauty on Boston Road the other night, I picked him up and he lived across the Bridge he said he had to be home early and would meet me 8.30 Friday night well as my luck goes, he didn't shine. "oh well"? Do you know its been about two weeks since I mopped?

Yours, Joe

Several of the bars also served as meeting places to pick up "trade" or "johns." "Trade" mostly referred to a straight or straight-acting male who was interested in sexual interaction with the same sex. "Johns" were paying customers who hired the queens for sex or companionship and sometimes both. The trick room, as previously described, was a safe place to bring trade for a date as the queens often did. A john would typically bring a queen to a hotel room or, on rare occasions, to his apartment. For the most part, johns were closeted married men and rendezvous were high risk for both parties, and therefore relegated to the shadows.

Joe, GiGi, Charlie, and Josephine appeared to be out for a good time with little-to-no-strings attached. Their primary focus was the conquest along with some friendly competition regarding who mopped on the most beauties and pulled the most trade. With this group, whoever was having the most sexual experiences won.

Dear Reno

Sunday nite I had the end scene with this norweigen fellow 6¾ Blonde 21 years old, you'll flip when I dish you the scene, I was over my sisters house sunday visiting when my Brother-in-law's nephew came over with 6 other fellow's to play Cards, I was sitting I n the living room when he came w and what a lump he had in his dungarees, I cracked, I started to dish with him about gay life, he said he never was Received by a boy, I'll skip the details and get down to the point, Well I asked him if he minded if I groped him, he said no, Wow what a piece of meat, I was getting all hot + Bothered, So I

started to go to town, and he
dug it to no end, he said
let me hold your head, and
banged me in the mouth,
how gorgeous it was, after we
finished he said he enjoyed it
very much and made a date
for next sunday.

Thanks for calling me sunday,
it was so good to hear your
voice again. You mopped in
two beauties, there were three
their, you know them, they
were at your house, one was
Tommy the blonde beauty but
he didn't get mopped in, she
asked me to come along but
I didn't want to go. Well I
guess thats about it Reno, I
can't think of anything else
to say. By the way this is
my 7th letter do you, I only
received 4 from you, your the
one that should write more
often, So git busy and write.
Take care of yourself.

    Your friend
    always.
    Charlie

love + kisses
xxxxxx
x — xx.

Dear Reno

Sunday night I had the end scene with this Norwegian fellow 6 3½ blonde 21 years old, you'll flip when I dish you the scene, I was over my sisters house Sunday visiting when my brother-in-law's nephew came over with 6 other fellows to play cards, I was sitting in the living room when he came in and what a lump he had in his dungarees, I cracked, I started to dish with him about gay life, he said he never was pleasured by a boy, I'll skip the details and get down to the point, well I asked him if he minded if I groped him, he said no, "wow" what a piece of meat, I was getting all hot + bothered, so I started to go to town, and he dug it no end, he said let me hold your head, and banged me in the mouth, how gorgeous it was, after we finished he said he enjoyed it very much and made a date for next Sunday. Would you believe it while they were playing cards in the kitchen I was mopping in the living room. I took some chance, but it was worth it. Excuse some of the mistakes, but every time I think of it I get carried away. Thanks for calling me Sunday, it was so good to hear your voice again . . . Take care of yourself.

Your friend always Charlie

Love and kisses xxxxxx

Xxxx

Charlie had a mouth on her which often got her into trouble. God help you if she found out your weakness, because she would go in for the kill. Creating drama and stirring the pot was a specialty she served daily. Joe "the Beak" was always in the crossfire. In fact, the Beak was a name she proudly gave Joe, due to his prominent nose. (He detested that nomenclature.) Charlie thought of herself as "Queen of the Streets" and when Reno left for New Orleans, she placed herself in that position, even if it was all in her head.

Deep down, Charlie was hurting. The years of abuse and bullying from others caused her to build an invisible wall around herself as protection from the world. Throwing the first punch—verbally or physically—is what Charlie felt she needed to do, against the constant barrage of hate from a cruel society that inhibited her daily life. She couldn't hide the fact she was gay, making it impossible for her to blend into society; she was often turned down for regular employment. Businesses wouldn't hire queers, so it was impossible for effeminate boys and obviously gay males to find suitable employment.

Charlie put herself out there and forced her way into different groups, seeming to be everywhere at once. She was too much for the streets and often found herself in new dramas with trade and johns. She was a known prostitute in the town of Mount Vernon where she grew up and was often sought by local police for her sexual deviance and criminal behavior.

December, 1957

Well Rose I still am not working, it seems I can't find myself a job, and my father is boiling because I have not found one yet.

This is going to be a very short letter, because there's not anything else to dish about. So get busy with that mad pen, and start writing. So long until my next letter.

> Your Friend Always
> Charlie
> PS. We have nine inches of snow.
> It was a real blizzard. Xxxx xxx

This discrimination was the same for butch lesbians or anyone who visibly transgressed the binary, if not through their clothing, then through their mannerisms, voice, or demeanor.

There were some Samaritans that might hire queer people, but job prospects were limited. Daphne was a hard worker and employed at the Department of Transportation in the day, before working at the 82 Club in the night hours, but her paycheck wasn't enough to support her drag. So, she turned to sex work because it had already been normalised by her friends and because she needed to support herself and her expensive drag persona. Sex work was a necessity for some of the writers because it was a relatively reliable means of making money.

September 24, 1957

Dear Reno,

Please try forgiving me for not writing sooner. As usual, I've been in pretty much the spin. I've been working late almost every night, and then fly home for the television scene as usual. I'm typing this letter at work, and the only reason I'm not writing it out in long hand, is to fool my boss. (He thinks I'm doing my regular work).

I'm glad you reached your destination all right, and I really flipped over that soilder scene. It gave me that "far away places" yen. Especially the way things have been around here lately. The same old scenes if you know what I mean.

About a week and a half ago, Joe from Mount Vernon called me up and asked me if I wanted to go up there. I think it was a Friday night. He came over my house and picked me up. (I was thinking in terms of a Chris scene.) Well when we finally got up there Chris was there all right, but so were about fifty numbers. That diner was really jumping. We met Charley when we got there and went inside for a coffee seene. Remember that beauty Ace? Well he was back in town. With a rubish cunt he said was his wife. Sweet, but about fifty pounds heavier than her husband. He digs Josephine. He aseked about her, and you of course. They all asked about you. I told them you were in New Orleand. It sounds more glamourous than Alexandria if you know what I mean. Like who ever heard of Alexandria. Besides the rubes that live there. I'd like to mop on some of those rubes incidently.

I've been sort of doing a steady scene with a number from Jersey. I meet him every Sunday at the Bali. I only mopped once. The end Meat. If the scene is off for the buns though, I'm calling it off. It's been going on for about four weeksp now, but its not reall the scene I've been dreaming about. That soilder in Agusta sounds more like what would have been a sure fire cure for my general melencoly.

I haven't been seeing too much of Billy. She's in the same spin with henny. She's staying at Richards house now. I met her Saturnday afternoon at work. After we left, and were walking on 57th street, who do we meet but Hank. Well did he look rubish. He lost much weight and his eyes looked as us in a batz stare. Like he was on dope or something. I think he was. We had coffee with him and then flew. Billy said she wasn't even bothered with him anymore. However I know he doesn't feel the same way. I met him in front of the Stanwood's Friday, no Saturday , and he wants to get in touch with Billy. You know who else was in front of the Stanwood ? The same bulls that pulled the scene on us. I shit. They looked at me but didN't say a word. I flew so fast I did'nt give them a chance.too. Incidently, I didn't even mop that night in the mountains. There were too many numbers around. Charley made a sneaky date with Chris for me. We were supposed to meet him in like an hour by some demented bridge around there. However, he never showed up. Do you think I should try Ban the new dedderant that rolls on ? Maybe he just doesN't dig me. I went to the Bars all painted this weekend. I got passed the door at Arty's and showed them jerks what a real one looks like. The night of the Mount Vernon jaunt, Joe drove me back home. Charley came too. When we got to my house it was pouring cats and dogs. We bought coffees at a restaurant around my way., and sat in the car and dished for about an hour. We spoke of the weiderst things. You know, "Big meats i have had", and that sort of thing. "Rubes I Have Met" was antother entry. I held the floor in that one.

Baker (Josephine) was with me at the Bali Sunday night. I was with my number from Jersey, We all danced and danced, and danced and danced and danced and danced. My number has to catch a 12 o clock bus at 42. So he flew at about 11;30. At got vary boring, so me and Baker cruised the streets a while. I felt bummy and Wixit I didN't feel like going home to bed to prepare for the work the next morning. That is, until the next morning. I was dead. Well let me tell you what happened. We spot this hot looking blond ont the corne of the Bali. He looked at as and did one of those famous retakes. We started to fallow him He stopped at a store window. I got one of my now renouned famous vibrations. So Baker took my advice and we madexx an about face. All of a sudden he starts following us. I said herec's where Daphne gets knock number seven hundred and twenty two. This time me and Jo stopped by a window. He passed us and stood by a doorway. We couldN't read him for shit. Baker said let s dish. I did no volunteering. So she asked for a cigarette. He was much smiles. We cracked. He said he was looking for a good time. Well my dear, you never saw two party girls go into action so fast. He said he never did the scene beford. We flipped. We took hem to Joey Ferrara's place. Naturally he insided on walking behini. We did'nt exactly look like any of his college chums. We finally got to Joey's building on 74th St. We go up the stairs. We reach the top floor,where she lives. And there's about twelve maniacs roaming around up there. Some creep from the Cork asks me who the creep is. A frieni of ours, I said. Then he asks us for some pills. Baker flips. Then he asks the number for some pills. The number says- " I don't smoke." Daphne flips. The number was starting to get bugged and nervous xxt at the same time. So did I. Then we knock on Joey's door. A demented queen in a Gstring answers. The number practically passes, out. She was mopping on another number. " Joey ain't here she says. He went down to pick up a John" She closes the door. Josephine makes the slighest suggestion. She touches the number by the arm, hinting that she wanted to mop in the tearoom . He got so bugged. This is where it comes I said. He flies down the stairs. He yelling much apoligies. He spit on the floor. Gay? O well, I always say everything happens for the better. We didn't mop that night. Any crazy stories he must have ever heard about the " twilight men", were all re-enacted in less than ten minutes. I guess he'll never know what the scene is about xxxxnow. If he was a lil, he could have made the prize pinch of the centxxry. I'm sure he would have made Captain.

The biggest dish around town now is drag. I mopped on a platinum white wig. Its a cap wig. But the hair is long and the end. It costs one fifty. Baker took me to a place and we pulled the scene. She wants me to have it worked on. You know, have a lace put on and all. It needs alitta adding on the bottom for that Jayne look. If I douch it up, it'll really be the end. I'm still debating wheter or not to pull a scene. Billy hasn't got a place yet. If she does'nt get one., she won't be able to make me a dress. Bakerss having one made my Jacket Morell's dressmaker. The fags are going all out this year. Many beaded sheaths and things. If I can't pull the end scene, I'm not pulling any at all. It looks like Billy isn't going. Kenny. If she doesn't go, I don't feel like either. She was very upset incidently, that she didn't see you before you took off.

I'm hoping you are in fine health and good spirits when this Autobiography arrives. I'll try to write you again as soon as I get a chance, and have some more News. Josephine wants to write you too. I have to get her address. I'll send it to you if you don't have.it. Let Me Know.

Ja dee da —
fu now

For
as always

Daphne

Sept 24 1957

Dear Reno

We spot this hot looking blond on the corner of the Bali. He looked at as and did one of those famous retakes. We started to follow him. He stopped at a store window. I got one of my now renowned famous vibrations. So Baker took my advice and we made an about face. All of a sudden he starts following us ... He was much smiles. We cracked. He said he was looking for a good time. Well my dear, you never saw two party girls go into action so fast. He said he never did the scene before. We flipped. We took hem to Joey Ferrara's place. Naturally he insisted on walking behind. We didn't exactly look like any of his college chums. We finally got to Joey's building on 74th St. We got up the stairs. We reach the top floor, where she lives. And there's about twelve maniacs roaming around up there. Some creep from the Cork asks me who the creep is. A friend of ours, I said. Then he asks us for some pills. Baker flips. Then he asks the number for some pills. The number says—"I don't smoke." Daphne flips. The number was starting to get bugged and nervous at the same time. So did I. Then we knock on Joey's door. A demented queen in a G-string answers. The number practically passes, out. She was mopping on another number. "Joey ain't here she says. He went down to pick up a john." She closes the door. Josephine makes the slightest suggestion. She touches the number by the arm, hinting that she wanted to mop in the tearoom. He got so bugged. This is where it comes I said. He flies down the stairs. Me yelling much apologies. He spit on the floor. Gay? O well, I always say everything happens for the better. We didn't mop that night. Any crazy stories he must have ever heard about the "twilight men", were all re-enacted in less than ten minutes. I guess he'll never know what the scene is about now. If he was a lil, he could have made the prize pinch of the century. I'm sure he would have made Captain.

La Dee Da for now—Love—As Always, Daphne

I understand the impulses that led the queens to sex work, because I can personally relate to each one through their writings, though our journeys were different.

In 1984 I was a sophomore in high school. Ms. Hastings, who taught sexual education, began the class discussing the topic: Sexually Transmitted Diseases. During class, she turned her focus to a new little-known STD called: Acquired Immune Deficiency Syndrome, otherwise known as AIDS. She started the topic with a disclaimer letting us know this STD wasn't part of the curriculum and she wasn't technically allowed to discuss this in her classes because our school board had deliberately rejected its inclusion. She went on to explain to us that, as an educator, it would be a disservice not to inform her students of the risks of all STDs.

I can see Ms. Hastings in my mind turning the rods attached to the mini blinds as she closed them. Shutting out the rest of the world as to tell us was something that could potentially get her dismissed from her position. I remember her lowering her voice to be less audible (as though some government agency was going to bust down the door to our classroom and drag her away) as she began to tell us about AIDS. She informed us this disease was primarily killing homosexual males; it was transmitted through sexual contact with same-sex partners and could be transferred with bodily fluids.

They hadn't coined HIV—Human Immunodeficiency Virus— then. There was little knowledge and a lack of research about this disease and the Federal Government under Ronald Reagan our Republican president, refused to recognize its existence and wouldn't approve Federal funding to find a cure. People called it "the Gay Disease." There was a kid in my class who would stand up in the lunchroom and call me all sort of homophobic slurs, but the one that has stuck with me all these years, is when he asked me if I knew what the word G-A-Y stands for? GOT AIDS YET? America didn't know a whole lot about this disease, but one thing was sure, if you got AIDS, you died. There was no vaccine.

Reading these letters, it's easy to assume these queens were free spirits without too many concerns. The letters pre-date the AIDS epidemic by some twenty-five years and the idea that sexual activity could put their health in serious jeopardy or have a fatal risk attached wasn't a thought in their young minds. They had never faced a life-threatening pandemic in their community, so they had few health concerns about unprotected sex. Risks were in the consequences they faced every day by being themselves. In the end, it was their need to be wanted, to belong, to be valued and loved that prevailed and this outweighed the dangers.

I was fifteen and like most boys my age, constantly thinking about sex. I wasn't just fantasizing about girls either. I knew there may be a possibility I could be one of these homosexuals Ms. Hastings was talking about. I agonised over what it might mean for me, for my family, for my life. Would I die of AIDS, too?

The rest of the hour under Ms. Hastings' tutelage was spent learning about recognizing symptoms and how people died. She even told
us that many doctors would not treat AIDS patients for fear of contact. I left class that day with a dark cloud of fear and the unknown
over my head. Sex terrified me. I was having sex (with girls) and
always used condoms. I wasn't afraid I would get her pregnant, I was
afraid I would get AIDS.

I graduated high school and went on to college still with that crip-
pling fear. Looking back, I now realize I stayed in the closet longer
than I should have not just because of my faith and fear of persecution, but also the fear of contracting AIDS.

I began to have sexual experiences with same-sex partners during
the tail end of the AIDS crisis in the 90s. The ghosts and echoes of

that period and the generation we lost never left us, reminding us that stigma was still present, and AIDS had not been eradicated. Naturally, this impacted the kind of sex queer people were having during this period. It was tame and limited. We felt unable to have sex as freely as the generations before us. For instance—this is a rather crude example, but it hits home—in the 90s, very few people would admit to being a "bottom"—a person who prefers to receive anal penetration. Why? Because receiving anal sex felt more dangerous than penetrating, and we were afraid for our lives. All sexual interaction was fear based and also encompassed the shame and guilt that you put your life at risk. Days later, if you developed a dry cough or woke up sweating through your T-shirt (both symptoms), you were convinced you'd contracted the disease. This was a very real thought that every gay man, and a majority of queer people, struggled with during this time.

When going out on a first date, somewhere in the conversation THE BIG QUESTION was undoubtedly raised, "What's your status?" You had to treat every sexual partner as though they were positive for HIV. You would go with your partner get tested, wait two agonising weeks before your results were ready and the two of you would go to get your results together; until that happened, you used condoms. During the 90s when you did date someone serious, eventually you would get around to sexual intercourse, but it wasn't immediately on the menu. That was the way it was. The fear was real with every sexually active American. We had to conform to the times, or we would be subject to the cruel fate of the generation before us, who didn't have any foresight of the way sex and relationships would have to change, almost overnight. Personally, I feel this should not be taken for granted.

This feeling that sex was dangerous, or subversive, played into later experiences. Not long after moving to L.A., Robbie and I discovered a local bar which was a Hollywood institution. Numbers was a well-known restaurant/bar on Sunset Boulevard next to Greenblatt's Deli. The entrance was behind the building off the parking lot. Inside, a curved staircase lined with vertical floor-to-ceiling mirrors led you down to the main floor. The lighting was low with candles in the center of tables topped with starched white tablecloths adding to the ambiance. Numbers was a classy bar scene. Well-dressed older men would attempt to impress the younger men by buying them an expensive steak and lobster dinner. Robbie and I joked it was the "Hooker Special" (surf and turf). Numbers was a hustler bar, and the older patrons were gay Hollywood elite, producers, politicians, and closeted celebrities, otherwise known as the velvet mafia.

Tim and Steven were friends and older than Robbie and me by about twenty years. Tim was rugged, but polished. His blue eyes and black hair made him look exotic and we hit it off immediately. Robbie took a shine to Steven. They were both handsome men and I would have been interested regardless of the situation, but that night we were on a mission. Within five minutes of meeting, Steven explained to us that his partner was away for the weekend and if we were interested, he and his friend would like to invite us to his home for a nightcap. Apparently, these two were on a mission as well! Are we really doing this?

"All I Wanna Do" by Sheryl Crow was playing on the radio as we drove past the massive estates and mansions set back from the palm-tree-lined streets of Beverly Hills. Yes, we are really doing this. Robbie and I gave each other permission to play the scene out. Having no idea what to expect, we felt safe because we were experiencing the thrill of it together. In my car, on the way to the stranger's home, we made a promise out loud that we would have no shame from what we were about to do. We were nervous but being together gave us the strength to follow through with the new role we cast ourselves in as professional high-class hustlers. Somehow playing a role made it easier for us to accept the nature of the situation.

I pulled my Jeep Cherokee onto the gravel driveway and parked in front of a sprawling modern mansion. The double front doors were easily ten feet high, and Robbie and I shot a look to each other as we entered the home.

Black marble floors appeared to go on forever beyond the foyer and throughout the beautifully designed space. I could see the lit landscape of the property through the glass of floor-to-ceiling windows. The glowing blue of the swimming pool grabbed my attention as steam danced across the surface of the water. Behind me, I could hear Robbie joke with the host, "I LOVE a living room you can land a plane in." Soft instrumental music began to play on the sound system, filling the rooms. It wasn't long before Robbie and I were separated, and I could hear his voice fading away and a door close shut beyond the long corridors. I was alone with Tim, and I turned my attention toward him.

That evening, I played my role perfectly. I felt powerful and in control. I could feel this man's desire for me, and it was unlike anything I had experienced. Someone wanted what I had to give, and I liked that feeling so much so, I wanted more.

I wanted what I didn't receive in my childhood, and that was to be loved, and to feel protected. Looking back, I didn't realize I was seeking a father. Robbie, on the other hand, like Josephine, loved the cash and figured if he was having sex he might as well get paid.

It is easy for me to understand the behavior of the letter writers. Decades before us, they were seeking the same attention and surviving the only way they knew how. It is no surprise young LGBTQ+ people turn to sex for validation. I equated sex with love because I had no idea what healthy love felt like.

Eventually, I started hustling because someone gave me attention for what I had to offer. As a result, I sought validation from men— even if it was for a moment. The exchange was transactional, and I was aware of what I was getting myself into, but my yearning to fill the vacant space inside my mind took over and, at that time in my life, was worth the risk. I felt wanted and for someone who never felt as though they belonged, this was at the very least "something."

I felt stronger when I was with Robbie. Our sisterhood felt like it protected me from harm, though of course this was delusion. So was it for the queens in the letters.

One evening, Daphne and GiGi made their way to Central Park to meet up with some trade GiGi knew from her neighborhood. Central

Park was a good place to meet trade as there were fewer people around at night, so from their experience there was a good chance they wouldn't have a run-in with the police.

The drag ball was coming up and all the queens were stepping up their game to help alleviate the costs of their increasingly expensive hobby. Daphne was determined not to be the ugly stepsister and refused to be seen in a hand-me-down gown that had already made its debut—she would never hear the end of it! Even though Daphne didn't particularly like the crowd GiGi hung out with, she was strapped for cash, so finding a john was necessary for her.

The night was on the chilly side and Daphne was thankful she was wearing the black fur shrug that appeared one day in the trick room to keep her warm. The old streetlamps lining the winding paths through Central Park weren't lit, causing the park to appear darker than usual. Daphne pointed out her observation to GiGi, who seemed nonplussed, so she didn't think much of it either as they passed shadowed faces while walking past the Puppet Theater toward their destination. Observing these two arm in arm, an onlooker would naturally think it was just a couple of girls giggling and gossiping as they walked briskly by.

They met up with GiGi's friend by the public restroom. He was with another chum, and it was obvious they had been drinking. Daphne was used to drunk boys and it only meant she had to work harder. Daphne and GiGi followed the boys into the empty restroom. Inside, the boys' disposition changed, their language becoming insulting and their physical advances more forward. Daphne detested outward advances from trade when it wasn't on her terms.

Deciding this wasn't going to work, Daphne turned and grabbed GiGi by the arm and in her best Pig Latin she told GiGi, "We need to leave." *"Eway Eednay otay eavelay."*

At that moment, one of the boys grabbed Daphne by the neck and forced her into a stall as the other boy attempted to do the same with GiGi. Daphne screamed and began to fight back. The boy was much bigger than Daphne and threatened her, and she heard GiGi being hit across the face and falling to the floor in the stall next to hers. Daphne was forced to her knees in front of her attacker. In this moment she turned to survival.

"Ogay alongyay ithway ityay." "Go along with it," she yelled out to GiGi who was crying and pleading with the trade not to hurt them.

The boy began to pull open his belt and unfasten his trousers while pushing them down past his knees to expose himself. Daphne yelled out again to GiGi, *"Ietay ishay oelacesshay ogethertay!"*

"Tie his shoelaces together!" GiGi responded, *"Ullpay eirthay antspay ownday otay ethay oorflay!"* "Pull their pants down to the floor!"

Daphne did just that. With their pants down around their ankles the boys were pushed back against the wall, falling onto the tiled floor next to the toilet. This provided a moment of respite, as the two queens were able to open the stall doors and rush out of the restroom while their attackers struggled to stand. Because their shoes had been tied together this proved slow and cumbersome.

With their hearts beating fast and makeup smeared, Daphne and GiGi ran across the Great Lawn in their ripped stockings, holding their heels in a desperate attempt to get far away, as quickly as they could. This was a near miss and an undeniable warning.

Daphne grew tired of the whorehouses and hustlers on 42nd Street. Drunk men slumped up against buildings, as dealers stood in the doorways. Degenerates pawing at prostitutes in the shadows, negotiating over a few bucks. What was once thrilling and exciting became less so as the years passed.

The scene was waning, and reality began to settle in as horrific images began to occupy her thoughts. Frightening scenes of her friends taking hits across the face or a punch in their stomach intruded on her thoughts. Fear was becoming too real as time was closing in and perhaps next time, she wouldn't be so lucky, as she was that cold evening in Central Park with GiGi. Images of that encounter played over in her mind like a nightmare on a loop. As much as she tried to push away the memory of that night, she knew she would never be able to forget.

Friday November 15.

Dear Reno:

Reno, it was two nights ago that I started this letter. I started typing it a work and didn't get a chance to finish it. Well here it is Friday morning at work again. I got here at 8 o clock this morning and I'm running out of work, so now is the only chance I'll probably get, to proceed with this documentry. I usially get to work at ten. This morning we get a demented phone call at my house at five in the morning. My father's sister died/ My mother was all upset; and afraid to tell him. He didnót wake up till about six. It was a very unexpected scene, when she dished him. I could'nt go back to sleep, so I came to work. They both flew in a cab up to the bronx where she lived. These scences we have to all expect. I don't know what kind of a weekend I'll be having this week.

Listen I heard that there was much the Tornado bit in Alexandria. Did it effect you any? I hope not. Reno, Joey's blowing her stack. She wants that book back. Everybody and her mother read it. I hate to send it inó the mail. Maybe I can stall her off. I don't see her that much anyway. I want to have some new pictures of myself (butch) taken. I was thinking of doing the studio scene. I'll send you those when I do. Camille's on the same kind of kick. It's easy doing the whole butch scene if you have someone doing it with you. Somebody who was just as batz as yourself. And as long as you stay away from the boomattzas you don't feel your missing much. Here's another example of nervousness. I met Josephine the Sunday after the drag. She was very depressed and called me up for a get together and dish scene. Well I met her on 42. She as always was too much for the streets. A click of real gavones started follwing us on about 44thSt. We walked up to McGuiness's restaurant. That's right next door to the dance hall where Barbard works. Used to should say. I don't know what the hell happened to her incidently. Well anyway, I said Josie lets go into the restaurant and we'll shake them. There were about five of them.. I was shitting. So was Joe. They did'nt follow is in. Thank God. All of a dudden I spot a side door exit. Let's fly through that Josie I said. Well we go hurrying out the door and the trade are right out side. Mary we both shit! Then I did the famous camp of turning around looking back into the place pretending we were with more people. We stood there frozen in the doorway for about ten minutes. The trade just stood there not saying a word. Finally theif good will ambassador comes ofer to dish. The famous camp. " Do you Know Ricky Fangoola ? or something like that. No. Are youse both qeer ? Josephine--"Yes) Then I heard one whisper about "bread". Much fatch dishing. Finally I said well we gotta go now. We start walking to the corner. They shayed by the restaurant door. We no sooner get to the corner when two more numbers come walking from across the street. These two were from my neighbohood. Rubes ! They were looking for carfare or something. Luckily we gave them a bareg. We told them the trade behind us by the Restaurant were with is. The Camp. But it worked. Mary we flew up Broadway into the crowd. What a workout. Like this I don't need anymore. You know what I mean? Josie was the one they spoted. And a few months ago it wdould have been me. For what?

Listen before you come back home Reno try to same some money. Don't come back broke . The job situation is very next right now. I wanted to quit mine because My pay without overtime I can get anywhere. But from what I hear I'm staying put. There s nothing to be had. I can't see how you'll save money if you got through with the Face scene. Maybe you can hitch on to one of them Texas oil-well numbers.

Joe from Mt Vernon was supposed to call me last week butdidn't. One more dish. I wound like you now. Did I tell you the time I was coming home from work and met a number in a car around my neighborhood who I mopped on in a Lumber Yard ? Well I met Him again late the other night. The 69 scene was on. He's so buchch, that Its a camp. Actually He's fighting the gay scene. He's really in love with his close buddy who is in the Airforce. If you think your in a spin, or myself for that matter, you should have got a load of his dish. The things that go on in some circlesof straight life are enoughto make ours look prudish. There s so many frustrated straight numbers walking around. I wish I'd meet more of them though. That number that I' was going with from Jersey has become like horseshit. He s always around. No glamour. I hope you'll save money. I hope you'll pardon all the crossouts and errors on this letter. The reason is that I'm typing it just as fast as I talk. And as you already know, that's prettxy fuckin fast.

I've really got to be signing off now. I'm getting typist's cramp.

With all this dish about sensibleness and all, I want you to know that no matter what my appearance may be now, and that no matter whosoever I shall choose as my new companions, I reamin ------

                    As Always ,

Friday November 15, 1957

Dear Reno

I met Josephine the Sunday after the drag. She was very depressed and called me up for a get together and dish scene. Well I met her on 42. She as always was too much for the streets. A click of real gavones started following us on about 44th St. We walked up to McGuiness's restaurant. That's right next door to the dance hall where Barbara works. Used to I should say. I don't know what the hell happened to her incidentally. Well anyway, I said Josie lets go into the restaurant and we'll shake them. There were about five of them . . . I was shitting. So was Joe. They didn't follow is in. Thank God. All of a sudden I spot a side door exit. Let's fly through that Josie said. Well, we go hurrying out the door and the trade are right outside. Mary we both shit! Then I did the famous camp of of turning around looking back into the place pretending we were with more people. We stood there frozen in the doorway for about ten minutes. The trade just stood there not saying a word. Finally, their good will ambassador comes over to dish. The famous camp. "Do you know Ricky Fangoola? Or something like that. No. Are youse both queer? Josephine "Yes.") Then I heard one whisper about "bread." Much fatch dishing. Finally, I said, "Well, we gotta go now." We start walking to the corner. They stayed by the restaurant door. We no sooner get to the corner when two more numbers come walking from across the street. These two were from my neighborhood. Rubes! They were looking for car fare of something. Luckily, we gave them a barrage. We told them about the trade behind us by the Restaurant were with us. The Camp. But it worked. Mary, we flew up Broadway into the crowd. What a workout. Like this I don't need anymore. You know what I mean? Josie was the one they spotted. And a few months ago it would have been me. For what?

As Always,
Daphne

The dangers of sex work can't be overstated. While many today know that sex work is real work, the stigma still exists. But sex is different today in the age of mobile apps. Digital connections are abundant in most cosmopolitan cities, especially New York. Queer people are given data, photographs and information that empowers them to find a partner, whether just for the night or for life. This freedom has allowed more safety and liberated LGBTQ+ people from having to do a potentially dangerous dance with a new lover, as partners can be pre-screened.

Sex and romance are now inescapably bound with technology. Today the newer generations explore sex without the fear of AIDS because of pharmaceutical drugs, which are accessible to the population through a prescription from a medical doctor. These drugs are used in suppressing the spread of the virus. It is important to know these drugs are not 100 per cent effective and many homosexuals and heterosexuals who experiment in risky sexual behavior can still risk contracting HIV and other viruses today. These drugs are not an antidote and should be used as a layer of protection with your sexual partners.

It is certainly worth pointing out that structural inequalities still face members of the LGBTQ+ community, which often manifest in desirability politics. Despite the discrimination policies written and supposedly enforced by apps, there are still many instances of abuse, especially for trans people and people of color. Sexual racism remains rife, as it was in 1950s New York, and it would be remiss not to mention that while all queens were marginalized due to their sexual deviance, some were double persecuted due to the color of their skin.

While the letter writers are fascinating individuals with an enormous amount of bravery, it is important to understand they were humans with flaws and prejudices that were informed by the culture of 1950s America. Racism and segregation are prevalent throughout American history and this practice was rife in the 1950s. Generally, racism was commonplace in both the white heterosexual and the white homosexual population.

Although our queens were a close, diverse group, the letters inform us white queens used derogatory, racist language against queens of color. This is an uncomfortable truth, but one we must confront in order to broaden our understanding of this countercul-ture and America itself during this period. Sadly, as much as white Americans have outwardly advanced the last sixty years toward racial equality and acceptance for Black, Indigenous, and people of color, inwardly racism is still lurking among us. Living a normal existence is more dangerous for a BIPOC than their white counter-parts. Add the stigma of homosexuality and sex work, double that. This remains the case today.

CHAPTER SIX

Romance

A s much as Daphne needed to survive, her letters indicate that she prioritized romance and hoped for a lasting relationship. Her tender references in the letter below to "much kissing and holding hands" in a budding relationship with a man called Bob, tells us she is looking for real connection at a deeper level.

Friday February 7, 1958

Reno Zambambamteen!

I'm supposed to be going steady with this number Bob from my neighborhood. Ella, I've had numbers that dug me, numbers that featured me, and others that were even lofty for me. But this one takes the cake. He calls me constantly, and when were together its much kissing me every two minutes, holding my hand on trains, busses, movie houses, lobbies and just about every where we go. To put it mildly he's demented for me. Much kisses and claiming he can't sleep or eat ever since we met. And Mary I love it. I never felt so cunty. I'm starting to like him more + more too. But I want to have my cake and eat it too. He's not at all hip about the gay scene. (bars + such)

February 7, 1958

Ella, I've had numbers that dug me, numbers the featured me, and others that were even batz for me. But his one takes the cake. He calls me constantly, and when we're together its much kissing me every two minutes, holding my hand on trains, busses, movie houses, lobbies and just about every where we go. To put it mildly, he's demented for me. Much kisses, and claiming he can't sleep or eat ever since we met. And Mary I love it. I never felt so cunty. I'm starting to like him more + more now too. But I want to have my cake + eat it too. He's not all hip about the gay scene (bars and such). I even tried to discourage him a bit. I told him I was an ex-drag queen. (Not so long!) He's not annoyed. Nothing I do is fatch in his eyes. Gay? I needed that kind of a lift I have to see him tonight. I actually miss him and his compliments whenever he's not around. He came upon me like a shot in the arm. The kind I needed!

As Always, Daphne

Daphne may not have realized it then but sharing her basic human and universal desire for intimacy was a form of expression. Seeking love and affirmation in the form of a sustained romantic relationship was the ultimate taboo. While much of the queer underworld, as respectable society would have perceived it, was glamorous and exciting, the reality of gay life could be lonely. While friendships thrived in the world of drag, few men could even conceive of a same-sex relationship. Gay activity was strictly for the night, for secret rendezvous, which most likely would never bleed into their respectable daily existence. Love often felt like a very distant challenge.

Dear Reno,
What happened to you are you ill, why haven't you been writing I haven't heard from you in about two weeks.
Did you recive my letters.
Joe Disked me she called you the other nite, and you were feeling very blue, and discusted with your Job does this mean that you are coming back home. Please let me know what you intend on doing I don't know what your plains are because you are not writing as often as you should.
What seems to be the trouble. Dish me and let me know what's going on.
By now you should have

received my other three letters.
The Dish about the Blonde
is all Steeighted Out "I Think"
I am not going to Worry
about it any more they have
to Catch me In the act first,
and I Assure you they Wont
Ren. I really Found love at
last, after all these years.
This is the real thing it's
not like the others I used
to Call my Husbands afters having
them Once, this really is Love,
I have found the man
of my heart, and it is real.

Dear Reno

Dish me and let me know what's going on. Reno I really found
love at last, after all these years. This is the real thing not like
the others I used to call my husbands after having them once, this
really is love. I have found the man of my heart, and it is real.

Daphne's personal yearning for love and romance was constant in
her writings. She put herself out there for this ideal but many of her
conquests didn't measure up to her dreams. The idea of meeting the
perfect man and living in a house with a white picket fence was a
dream beyond reach, but one she dearly yearned for. She certainly
wasn't going to find it on 42nd Street. If he existed, she would have
found him by now. Daphne decided to kickstart her love life and do
the next best thing, she would hook a john who could support her
and show her the finer things in life.

Taking the road of least resistance was acceptable to Daphne because her goal in life was to be at the party; how she got there was between her and the Creator. Stepping up her game, Daphne strolled into the elegant Regents Row bar one evening to meet up with Josephine and Billy.

Arriving early, the bar was empty except for a stylish woman with thick arched brows sitting with an elegant, dapper man in his late thirties, both sitting at a low table near the long bar. In an instant Daphne recognized the woman: Barbara Hutton, a New York socialite and heiress to the Woolworth fortune. Photos of her danced across the pages of the magazines Daphne purchased at the Five and Dime. Immediately, she felt self-conscious of her own brows that had recently been tweezed thin like Lana Turner's.

Fuck it, she thought as she lifted her chin and slowly strolled past the table. As she passed, however, she couldn't resist complimenting Barbara's beautiful eyebrows—it was almost an unconscious impulse, and one she immediately regretted.

She turned away, embarrassed at interrupting the pair, but Barbara struck up a conversation, asking Daphne's name and inviting her to join them: after all, a pretty girl should never be without a companion. Barbara introduced herself and her cousin Jimmy, otherwise known as James Paul Donahue Jr., a confirmed bachelor who, to Daphne's fortune, was also an heir to the Woolworth estate.

Josephine and Billy stood Daphne up that evening. It was a relief, as they may have ruined her chance encounter to mix with New York City's upper crust. Daphne considered herself the most sophisticated girl in the group, and that night she hit it off sensationally with Jimmy. Jimmy was slightly effeminate and much older than Daphne's personal taste, but it didn't matter because he was handsome and generous. No one could ever accuse her of being a fool. Daphne found her john!

During Christmas that year, Daphne was home one afternoon, back in boy clothes, looking out the window as a white limousine pulled up in front of his father's home. A chauffeur got out, walked around the car and opened the rear passenger door as Jimmy Donahue stepped out. He surprised Daphne by taking her to a jewelry store on Fifth Avenue. Daphne stood among the jewelry cases and peered through the glass at all the sparkling diamonds, rubies, sapphires, and her favorite gem of all, emeralds; necklaces, bracelets in every size imaginable and the most exquisite chandelier earrings in white gold with pearls! *Josephine would shit!* she thought to herself as she smiled.

Jimmy instructed her to pick out five gold rings of her choice! Later that evening at a bar in the Village, Jimmy asked her to pick out five of the most handsome boys in the room and give each of them a ring for Christmas. Daphne was only too happy to oblige as Jimmy sang out "The Twelve Days of Christmas" operatically in the background. Daphne was beaming from ear to ear as she received hugs and adoration from these perfect beautiful strangers.

"These rings are from Michael!" Jimmy gleefully rang out. Cheers erupted all around him, and Daphne in this moment, was the happiest she had been in as long as she could remember.

The queens' lives were peppered with glimpses into the upper echelons. The letter writers strived always for glamor, for status, for beauty, which they represented through their drag. However, on the odd occasion, these ideals were realized.

Baron Dimitri von Minenkoff was a wealthy, extremely generous married man in his late sixties; a sophisticated gentleman with an elegant flair. He had escaped Germany in the 1930s during the Rise of Hitler and found refuge in America. Upon arriving in New York, he made his way to Long Island where he purchased a large estate for his new wife.

Baron Dimitri Minenkoff had a secret; he loved being in the company of boys dressed as women. Every Friday in June, his chauffeur drove the Bentley into the city. Josephine, Billy, Claudia, and Pretty Boy Johnny waited on the street corner in the Village for the driver to pick them up and take them to Long Island.

The Baron's wife and daughter were on holiday in Europe for a month-long Museum Tour starting in Paris. Whenever his wife and daughter were away, he invited a group of carefully curated queens to dinner parties for himself, to feed his own secret indulgence. The exchange wasn't about sex as much as it was about wanting to reconnect to his youth. As a teenager, he belonged to an all-boy cabaret troupe touring German towns and villages performing musical numbers and skits. Dimitri would fantasize about being young with his rowdy friends from the troupe. One day, his military father caught Dimitri, dressed in women's clothing, passionately kissing another male performer from the troupe and young Dimitri was sent off to boarding school.

The old man stepped out of the gatehouse and struggled with the heavy scrolled iron doors as he slowly pulled them open to allow the car to pass through the entrance. Trees lined the long road and, in the distance, stood the stately gray stone mansion with its enormous columns, basking in the afternoon sun.

Claudia joked that she was going to check out some books, as she thought the house resembled the New York Public Library.

"As if you read!" Billy jibed.

Four servants stood in line by the entrance ready to receive this evening's guests. Claudia handed her bag to the one in charge.

"Be careful with that, it's valuable," she joked. She hadn't brought much, just her "drag bag" (two wigs, girdle, bra and makeup) because the baron provided each guest with what they would wear to dinner.

Laid out on their beds, in the beautifully appointed sleeping quarters, were expensive evening gowns with shoes to match. A slim box containing long gloves wrapped in tissue was placed next to a smaller box which contained clip-on earrings and a pearl necklace. Claudia held up her Chanel gown and spun in front of the mirror.

In the next room, Josephine helped Pretty Boy Johnny, her laugh echoing off the tiled bathroom walls as she surveyed Johnny's wolfishly hairy body. She grabbed a bottle of Nair and squeezed the foul-smelling lotion directly onto Johnny's back. The Baron, aware

of Johnny's hair issue, had provided the bottle of hair remover. He'd thought of everything. The Baron was a kind man. Even Josephine couldn't find it in her to mop from him, but as he'd gifted them all entire ensembles, she didn't need to.

The four queens spent the early evening styling their wigs and painting their faces. They zipped each other up, made final adjustments, then walked down the grand staircase to meet their host. After they'd taken their seats in the elegant dining room, the servants placed linen napkins onto their laps. Wearing white gloves, they silently moved around the table in unison, filling the crystal stemware and sweeping away used plates, before placing a clean one in its place.

The Baron was in the middle of a toast when the phone rang. A servant appeared and leaned down to whisper in the Baron's ear. "Oh?" Surprised, he stood up and excused himself. Moments later the Baron returned with the announcement that his wife and daughter had returned from Europe earlier than expected and were on their way from the airport.

Everyone in the house that evening kicked it into high gear! The servants rushed up the stairs and helped the queens out of their gowns and put the dresses on to hangers. Evening gloves were placed back in boxes and jewelry returned. The rooms were already being attended to as the queens made their way down the stair-case, through the front door and into the Bentley, which had been brought round.

As the car passed the heavy iron gates, Claudia looked out the back window of the Bentley at the old man from the gatehouse, and noticed he tipped his hat at her before closing the gates. Claudia slid her hand into the front pocket of her trousers and pulled out two crisp hundred-dollar bills.

CHAPTER SEVEN

Ballroom Culture

T he underground drag balls were the highest level of competition for queens to compete for the judges' scores, trophies, and audience adulation.

Drag balls date back to late-nineteenth-century New York. They were underground events largely hidden from the mainstream population who felt these venues were a denizen of perversions. However, a little bad press didn't hurt and by the 1920s balls had become even more popular. Fashion was taking a turn and a new style was on the scene; the "Flapper" look was in vogue. Gone was the Gibson hairstyle of long tresses piled on top of the head and layers of clothing fastened with rows of tiny buttons over a confining whalebone corset. In their place were short, blunt bobbed hairstyles and scandalous short, fringed dresses that didn't leave much for the imagination.

Queer people began flocking to the balls in droves, wanting to emulate this new style. The press continued to assert their opinion on the drag balls and accused the queer people who attended for starting the Great Depression in the 1930s. The drag balls began coinciding with the great Harlem Renaissance during the 1930s, when art, literature and culture began to flourish in the African American neighborhoods in Harlem.

Phil Black was a club promoter and the most widely known promoter for dances and drag balls. He began Harlem's famous "Fun Maker" Ball in 1944 and was considered somewhat of a celebrity among queer people in New York during the 1950s. Phil Black's balls were not to be missed, but there were a number of notable other events too. The Dayzee Dee Ball and The Art Students League Ball were among the more popular at the time, and each event could pack in five to six hundred guests.

The laws at the time did not allow for drag queens to congregate, except for one night of the year. The Masquerade Law, which declared it a crime to have your "face painted, discolored, covered, or concealed, or [be] otherwise disguised ... [while] in a road or public highway," was lifted to allow club promoters to rent a ballroom or theater, for one night only. This gave the queens in the city an opportunity to dress up in high drag and parade around showcasing their glamor. Judges decided who was the best dressed for the night. These balls were the perfect escape for our queens, giving them a real sense of community; they lived for these events, attending more than one a night. Queens came home from these events and immediately began designing their gowns for the following year.

OCTOBER 28 1957

Reno, I'm in such a demented spin right now. I just don't know where to turn. I want to go drag, I don't want to spend the money to go drag, I want to go pink tea, then when I see the pink tea bar scenes around here, I don't want to go pink tea. Plus I'm debating whether or not to go doing a " cleaning" scene on the brows. If I do, I'll be right back where I started from. And somehow I don't want to do that. My Jersey love scene is on a stick. He's a real whore. Goes with anybody at the drop of a pin. I was supposed to meet him yesterday (Sunday) I didn't even bother going out at all. I had much company and stayed home all day. I had a blond crew cut number with horse meat, a priceless lovemaker at Everol's. He was asking me many questions about where I came from and all that. He lives out in Hempstead LI. I was picturing the end love scene. After the sex scene, He says well I'll see ya around. I died ! You really can't expect any thing else from anybody you meet there. I was actually stupid to even think so. He would have been just the thing to convert me into a real home body.
Everytime I meet one of the boomatzas on the street they ask me what I'm wearing for Phil's. Its really getting me down. The temptation is becoming too great. Carmen told me she has a red wig to lend me. Then I heard a dish that it was fatch. The scene is, I've saved up nearly two hundred dollars, that I had intended to spend on drag. But now that I have the money, I think it would kill me to spend it on that. I was thinking of all the things I could do with it. Plus how much more I could do if I keep adding to it, instead of spending it and having to start all over, after the drag.
You know, I was contemplating , on doing the New Orleans scene for Mardi Gras. Billy is still hot for the idea too. If I save this money, the scene would really be on. I can take a whole month off from work in February. I was thinking if we flew out there on a plane, we might all be able to come

Josephine wearing a gown designed by Billy Norton

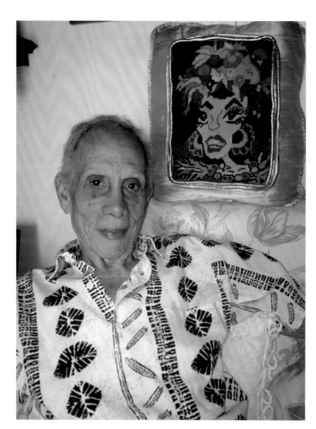

Henry "Adrian" Arango

Adrian with the severed
head of John the Baptist

Me and Robbie performing as
Marilyn Monroe and Jane Russell

Me as a mermaid on the back of
a Cadillac Hot Tub, LA Pride

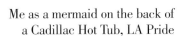

Club 82 full cast promotional shots

Michael Alogna as Daphne

Terry "Teri" Noel

Ed Limato and me

Mom and me holding my cat Axel

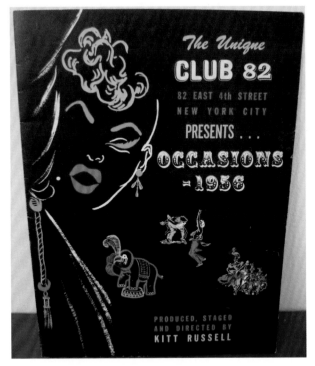

Club 82 Program

Club 82 promotional postcard

Billy Baker and Josephine

back togehter. That is if·you have still got the·intention of retruning here.
With all those bummy scnes, like that bar in Texas, New Orleans and all, I would
be in no rush whatsoever to get back here. Many things are really horrid !

I'm so fed up with everything. Everything piled up in my mind and broke
out in a crying jagg with me. I left Camille downtown Saturday night. I was
on the train going uptown. I·was going to do the Stanwood scene. As started
thinking is over on the train, I decided to get off at 42 and go home instead.
To put it plainly I'm disgusted with myself and my accomplishments. Which are
none. I walked from the station, to my house and broke out in a very un-gay
tear scene. I haven't done that in a long time. But its just the way I felt
and I couldn't help it. I felt a little better afte· it was over. But it still
hasn't helped my desperate situation any.

I really crack when I hear of all the gay places and gay happenings that
are taking place everywhree but where I am. I've come tox the conclusion that
your have to be the end gorgeous butch, to mop gayly in the pink tea set. Camille
has a·batz short haircut. She wants me to get the same. Like just to please
the pink tea rubes. But I can't stand myself with one of those demented haircuts
Remember how that sailor in Norfolk cracked over my Hair ? And he was gay too.
Those kind of numbers just don't happen around here. It's a rat race. All I
can keep hoping is " Someday He'll come along--" I still stick to my story that
ther's someone for everyone who wants them. And I'll just keep waiting. While
I'm getting older. (Another bugger)

About that big dark secret in you letter. Could it be a face sanding scene?
Or are you having the Christine operat·on. Nothing would come as a shock anymore.
I never know what you're going to pull next. I just hope that if and when you
do come back, you don't get demented again.

I remain as always,

Daphne

October 28, 1957

Dear Reno

Everytime I meet one of the boomatzas on the street they ask
me what I'm wearing for Phils. It's really getting me down. The
temptation is becoming too great. Carmen told me she has a red
wig to lend me. Then I heard a dish that it was fatch. The scene
is, I've saved up nearly two hundred dollars, that I had intended
to spend on drag. But now that I have the money, I think it would
kill me to spend it on that. I was thinking of all the things I could
do with it. Plus how much more I could do if I keep adding to
it, instead of spending it and having to start all over, after the
drag ... The crowd is going all out for this one you know. Baker
hasn't called me this weekend. She's undoubtedly in a spin for
Friday night.

I remain As Always, Daphne

The House of Boomatza, which included all the letter writers, was a sisterhood, as described by Daphne. "Chosen family" is a phrase commonly used by queer people today. Sisterhood and chosen family are the same thing, used to describe individuals who develop closer social bonds due to societal and biological family marginalization. (The phrase "chosen family" wasn't widely used until the late twentieth century.) As we know from the letters, Daphne and Josephine took these competitions extremely seriously and would do whatever it took to create a show-stopping ensemble. When reading the letters, you can feel the excitement and the dramas that ensued in preparation for each event, as well as the fallout after. In fact, in one extremely entertaining letter from Daphne she gives a commentary on how all the queens looked. No one is spared as she dishes about every Boomatza at an event from the night before and I dare say, could possibly be the first written "drag shade" in history!

November 13, 1957

Dear Reno:

As usual, all I can say is " Forgive me for not Writing sooner," but I honestly
mean it. I received your very bummish letters at Camille's house. Those scenes down
there are just too much for my condition. Joe told me that he has been writing you
about all the news from these parts, so I guess anything I would dish would only be
repetitious anyway. I got my biggest lift when I went to that so called " Drag". One
simple little word would appropiately sum up the whole affair. And that's NEXT !
It was the rat race of the year. On entering the Hotel, I said to myself, Gee this place
is so campy looking, that I should have come here and pull the scene, instead of going to
Phil's. Well I've definitely decided that I'm not pulling Phil's either. I'll telly you
why later. Tox start off with, there was no bummish trade there. The lighting was
horrible, the ballroom was small, and in general, a boring, sickening scene. With all the
familiar drag faces, looking disgustedly disappointed. Josephine lookedXX the complete
end. She came a little later than the rest. She walked in, expecting to crack the joint,
but nobody was bothered. She told me later that she was very bugged as was everyone else.
At any other affair, she would have brought the walls down. Her gold lame outfit with
matching coat, and buffont red hairdo, were really enough to win a prise at any drag. But
here, she was just one of the crowd. Jackie Morrell looked like she had it. She was
so tired looking, and seemed to be there because it was the expected thing. Nickelina.
If you saw her onees, as the old saying goes. She was wearing a white beaded sheath.
One more beaded sheath to add to her beaded sheath collection. Plus a black ponytail. (A
new scene.) Carmen wore the same hairdo. And a black dress. For a change '. D isy Dietz
wore pink chiffon. Very chic really. I cracked over her pink satin pumps. Johnny Boy
looked lik Johnny Boy in hers own hair and Cino's old aqua shiffon number. Kiva looked
like she just stepped out of the Everod steamroom. She wore a wet silver lame number, and
a little blonde hair, stringy with sweat. Tony L followed her around the place like a
lady in waiting. She wore "pink hair". The style was something like a floor mop worn upsi
down on the head, with a pink rinse run through it. Frankie said the looked like she
painted her head with glue, and then stuck Christmas Angel Hair on it. That should give
an adequate picture of it. Glaudia wore a gorgeous black fringe dress. A "Brooks Costumes
Original". Her wig was shit brown. Knotted in the back like a little brown turd.
Listen to this. Amber has white hair now as usual. Over it, she wore a pasty looking
brown*blonde wig. Next! As usual, Rudy looked like a sepia darling. Frankie and Georgae
came in smart ski-sweaters, searching for something warmer to walk out with. But it so
happened that nobody at thexxfaffair wore mink. So their attempts were futile, and extremely unsuccessful. Jet's girlffiad looked very sweet. I'm sure she would have had a much
better time at one of the High School proms. Kim Drawback, wore small strips. She had
to feel herself around the place. Did you ever see a broomstick in a full taffeta skirt?
The rexemblence was remarkable. These mind you were the "stars" of the show. Some of the
staflets were really priceless looking. The noses on some of them were enough to keep
a staff of plastic surgeons working day and night for mucho drags to come. Some of them
really have some balls to pull the drag scene And the shapes! A lot of them blamed
there appearance on the weather., It was pouring out. As Joe and I were leaving the place,
Alicia summed up the whole affair with a smart quip. " Two hundred dollars for this ! "
We didn't even have the pay the two dollar admission charge. They should have called it
a circus party. Because that's just what it looked like. We left with Steve and a friend
of his in drag, and went to a Pink Tea Halloween party. It was worse !
I knew immediately what you were dishing when you mentioned the scene you were going
to pull. I think that face sanding scene would be sensational. But really Reno, your face
was never that bad. And the way you described it's clearing up with just the medicine,
I think you should really think it over beford going. Actually that scene is like for
hopeless messes. And I understand it costs a lot too. It would be gay to talk to someone
who actually had it done beford making up your mind to go through it yourself. I saw a
woman in my neighborhood with it. The whole side of her face was like a huge saab. She
was in the healing process.
Another dish about the "Drag". I heard Marty telling some queen, " Do you know it
took Burma only an hour to whip me up this dress ? Queen's reply - "Did it really take
that long?/ The fatch. Caledonia looked like the leading lady of one of New York's most
famous night clubs. Sammy's Bowery Follies. I heard later on that when Kiva was leaving,
she was slightly drunk and took a huge flop in the hotel lobby. It took Tony L, with the
assistance of two strong armed hotel doormen, to lift herx, and load the load into a waiting
taxi. Kiva must have had about twenty yards of lame in her gown. It was a sheath.

As Always ,

Japhne

November 13, 1957

Dear Reno:

Joe told me that he has been writing you about all the news from these parts, so I guess anything I would dish would only be repetitious anyway. I got my biggest lift when I went to that so called "Drag". One simple little word would appropriately sum up the whole affair. And that's NEXT! It was the rat race of the year. On entering the Hotel, I said to myself, gee this place is so campy looking, that I should have come here and pull the scene, instead of going to Phil's. Well, I've decided that I'm not pulling Phil's either. I'll tell you why later. To start off with, there was no bummish trade there. The lighting was horrible, the ballroom was small, and in general, a boring, sickening scene. With all the familiar drag faces, looking disgustedly disappointed. Josephine looked the complete end. She came a little later than the rest. She walked in, expecting to crack the joint, but nobody was bothered. She told me later that she was very bugged as was everyone else. At any other affair, she would have brought the walls down. Her gold lame outfit with matching coat, and bouffant red hairdo, were enough to win a prize at any drag. But here, she was just one of the crowd. Jackie Morrell looked like she had it. She was so tired looking and seemed to be here because it was the expected thing. Nickelina—she was wearing a white beaded sheath. One more beaded sheath to add to her beaded sheath collection. Plus, a black ponytail. (A new scene.) Carmen wore the same hairdo. And a black dress. For a change. Daisy Diet looked like Johnny Boy in her own hair and cino's old aqua chiffon number. Kiva looked like she just stepped out of the Everod steam room. she wore a wet silver lame number, and a little blonde hair, stringy with sweat. Tony L followed her around the place like a lady in waiting. She wore "pink hair." The style was something like a floor mop worn upside down on the head, with a pink rinse run through it. Frankie said the looked like she painted her head with glue, and then stuck Christmas Angel Hair on it. That should give an adequate picture of it. Claudia wore a gorgeous black fringe dress. A "Brooks Costumes Original." Her wig was shit brown. Knotted in the back like a little brown turd. Listen to this. Amber has white hair now as usual. Over it, she wore a pasty looking brown*blonde wig. Next! As usual, Rudy looked like a sepia darling. Frankie and Georgie came in smart ski sweaters, searching for something warmer to walk out with. But it so happened that nobody at the affair wore mink. So, their attempts were futile, and extremely unsuccessful. Jet's girlfriend looked very sweet. I'm sure she would have had a much better time at one of the High School proms. Kim Drawback, wore small stips. She had to feel herself around the place. Did you ever see a broomstick in a full taffeta skirt? The resemblance was remarkable. These mind you were the "stars" of the show. Some of the starlets were priceless looking. The noses on some of them were enough to keep a staff of plastic surgeons working day and night for mucho drags to come. Some of them really have some balls to pull the drag scene. And the shapes! A lot of them blamed their appearance on the weather., It was pouring out. As Joe and I were leaving the place, Alicia summed up the whole affair with a smart quip. "Two hundred dollars for this!" We didn't even have the pay the two-dollar admission charge. They should have called it a circus party. Because that's just what it looked like. We left with Steve and a friend of his in drag and went to a Pink Tea Halloween Party. It was worse!

As Always, Daphne

All the Boomatzas entered competitions hoping to raise the bar. It didn't matter who won, as long as it was someone from within the sisterhood. They came together as a group and contributed as a family, using their individual talents and creativity when helping each other complete a "look" for the drag balls. Claudia did the hair. Daphne did the makeup. Josephine stole bolts of fabric and Billy created their show-stopping gowns. These events were highly competitive and standing out was the priority. These girls demanded a turn of the head on the catwalk at any ball, but most importantly Phil Black's Ball. The Boomatzas can be seen as a precursor to the current "houses" of modern-day ballroom culture.

November 20, 1957

Dear Reno,

Well it's me again. Star reporter of the N.Y.
gay set rat race. There was a fatch scene at my house
Friday. My father's sister died. We got one of those
x5:30 in the morning phone calls. It was my cousin giving
us the dish. It was much the demented scene. Yesterday
was the funeral. It was a very ruby scene, and I'm glad
its over now. I saw many cousins I hadn't scene in many
moons. And once again I was glad my eyebrows and everthir
were sensible. I was'nt worried about facing any of them
which made the whole affair a lot easier for me. I think
I made a gay impression on them. I thought I read one of
them giving me like the fatch. Evertime I'd catch him
staring at me, he'd like look away real quick. Maybe he
was reading. But I'm really not concerned about it anyway

Tony L was over Camille's Saturday night. I stopped
up there before going out. She was slightly painted.
The only thing she forgot were earrings. She said she
had to meet Georgie for a Brooklyn cruise scene. I know
you're hot for that scene, but all I could say was "KaFatc

I think IXIX I'll go to Phil's to cheer my sisters on
I'm eating Thanksgiving dinner at my Sister's I think.
I'm very curious naturally, to see the naid ball.

Do you want to hear something gay ? I was walking
on 6th Ave last week, and I met the photographer who took
those pictures of me at his studio last year. He said he
had been trying to get in contact with me. Some magazine
wants to do a layout on a complete drag scene. He said
they had chosen me when they saw my pictures. They want
a series of the whole "getting in drag" process. You know
Before and after. This was like the devil's temptation.
Had I consented, I would have upset all of New York again.
But that's such a risky scene. Someone I would'nt want to
know, would definitely get the "drag" dish about me. And
it might be my sister or brother or someone like that.
I was flipping, but had to say no to this very hard to
resist offer. It would have been the end scene, since all
the pictures would have been specially posed and everythin
This is like the real test of my big reform.

Zamboona I really have to sign off now. Once again
I hope this proclamation, finds you in good health and
fine spirits. I'll say so long for now, while I remain

As Always -

Daphne

November 20, 1957

I think I'll go to Phil's to cheer my sisters on. I'm eating Thanksgiving dinner at my Sister's I think. I'm very curious naturally, to see the naid ball.

As Always, Daphne

The balls of the 1950s were organized and modeled after traditional beauty pageants. Glamor and elegance were the priority. Since this period in American culture championed a hyper-feminized ideal of womanhood, the drag balls for the most part mirrored the binary image of a very glamorous female form of the day, full firm bust and hips with a small waist to look as real femme as possible. Trophies were awarded for best hair, gown, makeup, and overall head-to-toe look. As such, the performative aspects were limited to strutting, walking, and posing. The queen who displayed the most convincing approximation of conventional beauty, and considered to be most "passable," would invariably take home the coveted crown and trophy. Those who didn't fit this narrow definition of femininity were openly ridiculed. This was not a time when body positivity, or even body neutrality, was in the psyche. If you were deemed overweight or had stereotypically masculine features, the crowd would let you know. If a competitor was hairy or too tall or ran afoul of beauty standards in any capacity, they would be ridiculed.

Segregation in America was rampant, and white people did not mix with Black people. However, the drag balls and the crowds that came to these events were mixed. Black and white people came together in a non-clandestine way. All were welcome and all were accepted. It is quite remarkable when you pause on this notion; there was *no* segregation at the drag ball! Black and white queers danced together, laughed together, and competed together, and because these communities by large are inclusive, heterosexual men and women were also welcome. This was the first time in American history this came to be, and it happened at the drag balls.

"*You felt as though you 'belonged' at the drag ball, and it was a wonderful feeling, because you never 'belonged' anywhere before.*"
Claudio "Claudia" Diaz

"*Anyone who was Anybody came to the Drag. It was fun!*"
Terry "Teri" Noel

"*The balls were glamorous! All glamor queens, nobody wants to be glamorous anymore, they all want to be clowns.*"
Henry "Adrian" Arango

Inside the drag ball you would be in awe over the exquisite faces, and highly styled wigs that seem to float atop the gowns in a sea of satin and glittering diamonds. It was an elegant masquerade fantasy of glamor and style. Outside on the sidewalk, however, queer people were targeted, violence erupted and heterosexual onlookers, in a "rage against the gay," tore the gowns off queer people. Cops and security were paid to protect the people at these authorized licensed events, but when the event was over those same people could be excessively violent toward the glamorous patrons. Both Black and white homosexuals were targeted, and police brutality was common.

The queens took a tremendous risk to their safety when stepping out, but it was their resilience, their desire for community and the love of spectacle that encouraged them to come back year in year out.

Although it was mixed, the Black and Latin communities began to see racism in the competition. The judges were all white, and trophies were awarded to the white contestants even when it was clear by the audience reaction the Black and/or Latino contestants were better. Black and Latino communities were often overlooked when competing in the drag balls.

This discrimination didn't fare well with the Black and Latino communities and modern ballroom culture began to take shape. By the late 1970s ballroom culture was becoming a thriving subculture pioneered by Black and Latin individuals. Artistry and artifice grew, facilitated by an increased sense of safety and legitimacy. The New York balls were inclusive events that also allowed transgender and bisexual men and women to enter categories in drag. BIPOC lives thrived as art and culture merged with pageantry and people traveled from far and wide to attend. Queer youth felt accepted and individuals rose to prominence as celebrities or "legends" on the New York scene.

By the 1980s, vogueing was becoming a mainstay of the ballroom scene. Vogueing is a stylized dance that seeks to imitate the sharp poses of supermodels from fashion. The first truly global introduction to this art form came from Madonna in 1990, with her perennial

hit "Vogue." She brought voguing to an international mainstream audience and employed ballroom performers like Luis Camacho and Jose Gutierez for the Blonde Ambition Tour. However, by no means did Madonna create this style of dance, which was created and spearheaded by queer people of color, and she undoubtedly appropriated a culture that she had no right to lay claim to.

Today's ball competitions include the current categories defined by "Realness": Butch Queen, Femme Queen, and Executive Businesswoman to name a few. You have to "pass" or you don't score. Participants compete against each other on the runway in stylized dance battles with attitude! Spins and dips (also referred to as "death drops" in popular culture) are a mainstay in ballroom culture. These heart-stopping moves have been adopted by young queens in every city across America and always slay when used in perfect timing with the beat drop of the music—the crowds go wild! Ballroom culture has been appropriated into the mainstream and we now have reality shows which celebrate ballroom culture and celebrate BIPOC and trans people.

But we need to remember, none of this commercial success would have been possible without the early underground drag balls of the 1950s, which the letter writers describe with breathless enthusiasm. It is remarkable how, regardless of race, the resilience of queer youth ensures they find one another out of necessity and desire for acceptance. Their families may have been distant, disapproving, or worse, but the ballroom competitions and their comradeship made them feel appreciated and loved. Daphne sums it up best in a letter to Reno . . .

Once a Boomatza always a Boomatza!

CHAPTER EIGHT

Family

New York's Newest
and Most Unique Nite Spot

CLUB 82

TAKES YOU ON

A VACATION IN COLOR

(FOR AFTER-DARK DIVERSION SEEKERS)

PRODUCED BY

NEIL STONE

STAGED AND DIRECTED BY

KITT RUSSELL

New **CLUB 82**

82 EAST 4th STREET · GRAMERCY 7-1046

"NEW YORK'S MOST UNIQUE NITE SPOT"

presents

3 — SHOWS NIGHTLY — 3

10:30   12:30   2:30

FOR RESERVATIONS, CALL OUR MAITRE D' — CONNIE

Phone Reservations Number — GRamercy 7-1046

CLUB 82 is located at 82 East 4th Street, 4th Street & 2nd Avenue

A GLAMOROUS AND SPARKLING REVUE IN ONE OF THE
MOST BEAUTIFUL ROOMS IN DOWNTOWN MANHATTAN

O f course, the Boomatzas did not simply go to balls together. In the moralistic world of the 1950s, the need for family connection ran deep. Many of the letter writers had at best strained and at worst actively abusive relationships with their biological families. They needed alternative bonds to counteract this.

Claudio "Claudia" Diaz and Roberto "Josephine Baker" Perez were joined at the hip after meeting that evening at the Cork Club. Josephine immediately took Claudia under her wing and invited her into the underground world of New York. Having just turned fifteen, the impressionable Claudia was more than happy to accept any positive attention she could get from Josephine, because it was the first time in her life she had found a true friend. Their friendship grew and they became one another's extended family.

At home, Mr. Perez's patience was wearing thin. He could no longer control his son who seemed not to care about anyone other than himself. The disappointment grew into anger, as Roberto spent every moment he could away from home, sometimes even staying out all night. When suspicions began piling up regarding his son's proclivities, and when these rumors reached his doorstep, Mr. Perez was faced with the harsh reality that his own son was a homosexual who has been parading around the city dressed as a girl, calling himself Josephine! Mr. Perez's reaction was not unlike most parents'—he took it as a personal reflection on himself.

Not knowing where to turn and most certainly feeling backed into a corner, he confronted his son in a heated exchange, which resulted in kicking Roberto out of his home. Roberto's father would have gotten his way, had it not been for his mother's interference. She didn't understand her son any more than her husband, but she was a mother, and loved her son without prejudice. Mrs. Perez may not have agreed with what her boy was becoming, but she would be damned if she was going to allow her husband to take the lead in this instant.

Roberto, deciding he could no longer stay where he wasn't wanted, turned to his friend Claudio, whose life always seemed worse than his own. Together the two self-proclaimed misfits hatched a plan and ran away from home. The pair got on a bus and headed to Miami, where they hoped they could more easily blend in. Best of all, Miami was warm, and Roberto had heard through the "Gay Vine" you could make money very easily as a call girl there. As Josephine, she would take care of them both.

The gentle air tickled her face as it pushed through the open window on the Greyhound bus. Staring out of the window Claudia watched the landscape pass her by. She had never seen so many trees in her life! With every town they passed she felt she was able to breathe again, as though her grandmother's hands were loosening their grip from around her neck. She wondered if "the old hag" would even notice she was gone. She'd probably figure it out when she wasn't there to receive her daily beating. Claudia looked down at Josephine who was asleep with her head on her lap. Sitting on the bus traveling down the highway she felt safe, and this revelation put a smile on her face. She could hear the hum of the engine and feel the soft vibration of the bus causing her heavy-lidded eyes to gently close as she drifted off to sleep.

The bus pulled into a roadside diner and the two were awakened by the announcement from the driver, they were taking a forty-five-minute dinner break. Josephine popped up and looked out the window. Not much to see. Having to relieve herself after her nap she went to use the restroom at the back of the bus. Occupied.

"Where are we?" Claudia asked.

"Bumfuck," Josephine replied, as they exited the Greyhound.

Off the bus, Josephine walked around to the back and decided outside would be as good a place as any to take a quick piss. Mid-stream, the sirens went off and three "black and whites" pulled up with lights flashing. Claudia rushed to Josephine's defense.

Seeing these two Puerto Ricans with their eyebrows shaved off and a smear of eyeliner under their eyes, it was easy to assume they were not from around these parts. The officers on duty had no pity for the "sissy boys" and took it upon themselves to enforce their author-ity: handcuffing and taking them into custody. Neither of them was carrying identification, and it didn't help that the pair weren't being forthcoming with information as to who they were—neither one of them wanted to go back to where they didn't belong.

Josephine and Claudia found themselves detained in the state of Alabama. After two days in jail the officers—realizing they couldn't book them for anything greater than loitering—put them in the back of a patrol car and drove them to the state line, where they left them standing on the side of the road in the middle of nowhere. It wasn't long before another state trooper flashed his lights and pulled up alongside them. The officer rolled down his window, challenging them on how old they were and what they were doing. When Claudia and Josephine lied about their age, pretending to be seventeen, they found themselves detained again.

This time, however, it wasn't the luxury of the jail cell in

Alabama. They found themselves in a chain gang. Obviously queer, Claudia and Josephine were promised by the officers to the other inmates and forced to do sexual favors as a reward for their "good behavior." Claudia would lie awake at night in the long dark room she shared with the other inmates, staring up to the rafters. She only allowed herself to break down when the other inmates were asleep.

One morning Claudia looked out through the dirty window and saw a Black man hunched over, pushing a wheelbarrow across the compound. The man looked up, noticed Claudia peering out the window and stopped in the middle of the yard. He stood up with a big friendly smile and waved to Claudia. She waved back, when suddenly, to her horror, the man was grabbed by two guards and dragged to the perimeter of the yard. It was a rule that Black and white inmates were forbidden to interact. The man didn't put up a fight as the guards tied him to a fence and whipped him until he was unconscious and covered in blood.

Fearing she would be next, Claudia ran out into the compound in sheer terror screaming. "I'm fifteen!" she yelled over and over, "I'm fifteen!" She dropped to her knees, tears streaming down her face, "I'm fifteen."

That afternoon, Claudia was separated from Josephine and taken by bus to an airport to be sent back to New York. Claudia feared she would never see her friend Josephine again.

When Claudia landed back in New York, the large door on the airplane swung open to allow light into the cabin. As she stepped outside, her eyes adjusting to the bright daylight, she slowly made her way down the mobile staircase, and noticed her grandmother. She looked small from this distance, standing in her good coat, holding a white handbag. Her face was expressionless; nothing about her betrayed any hint of emotion at seeing her grandson return. She stared right through Claudia, who refused to look away, defiantly maintaining her gaze.

As she came within three feet of her grandmother, the old woman

pulled her arm back, holding her handbag tight, and hit Claudia upside her head with such force she fell onto the tarmac. She said nothing to Claudia while turning her back on her and walked away. Nobody did a thing.

Eventually, Claudia was lifted to her feet, her head still spinning from the blow, and put in the back seat of a black car. The vehicle transported her to Bellevue, a mental hospital. She was assigned to PQ5, the psych ward for violent, unmanageable boys—"the homosexuals." Claudia was closing in on sixteen and her traumatic ordeal—being wrongfully incarcerated as a minor, sexually abused and demeaned by the institution that was supposed to protect her— was far from over.

She spoke with a therapist daily and was questioned endlessly by a man who Claudia sensed was only there to collect a paycheck. She had given up all hope as the pain and anguish from this past year had clawed at her sanity and left her void of trust for any authoritarian.

But, in time, a psychologist sat down with Claudia, who considered the newcomer one more person not to trust. Rolling her eyes, Claudia defiantly spit out the words she had always been accused of but never had the courage to admit out loud, "I'm a homosexual," thinking this self-proclamation would put the doctor on the defensive.

The psychologist sat with this announcement for a moment before posing a question to Claudia, "What's wrong with that?" It wasn't so much a question—more of a retort, *So what?*

The years of pain, humiliation and fear Claudia had kept hidden inside, buried beneath her tough exterior, had penetrated the surface. It was all too much to bear as the tears ran down her face. Her body shook as she gasped for air to enable her to form the words and finally share her story with a stranger who was listening with compassion. The psychologist left a lasting impression that afternoon; he was the only adult who had ever shown kindness to Claudia, and in turn she would have followed this man into Hell for being kind.

"In my opinion it is your grandmother that should be here. Not you," he told Claudia.

Soon thereafter, Claudia was released from Bellevue and dropped off on the corner of Amsterdam and 125th Street. Claudia was on her own, but after what she had been through the last several months, she was unafraid. The only phone number Claudia could remember was Josephine Baker's.

Josephine could not contain her excitement as she, Daphne, Billie and GiGi all came to meet her. In a chorus of growing exultation, they circled around Claudia, taking up most of the sidewalk that afternoon. They hugged in a group, holding onto each other tightly, while wiping away each other's tears of joy. It was clear that the Boomatzas were bound together. Claudia was back! Regardless of the balls, of the tricks, of the catty fights, this was what sisterhood truly meant to the queens.

Years later, Claudia shared with me, "If it hadn't been for her friends, New York City would have buried five more queer youths."

Just like Claudia, there was no affection toward me in my home as a child. I was never told I was loved, and my parents' actions did not demonstrate it either. I was an effeminate little boy, and it was obvious I was different, which brought unwelcome attention to my family at church and with their peers.

My father considered himself a man's man and, in his eyes, I was a disappointment. His friends' sons were playing sports, but his own son had no coordination and zero interest in all the things he was interested in. He didn't know what to do with his gay son and sometimes I would catch him looking at me and I could sense him questioning, *How could my boy be so different?* I believe he wanted to relate to me but didn't know how, and it was easier for him to deal with his shame (or possibly his guilt) by ignoring me. He avoided me and in return I steered clear of him. I was afraid of my father because my mother taught me to fear him, using his alcoholism as a tactic. I was told to go to my room every night when his car pulled into the driveway. Her reasoning was "he could be drunk and violent." Being a little boy, I took this banishment personally; I feared, if my father saw me, I would remind him of his regret about me, causing him to drink more. I was under the assumption his alcoholism was because of me, and my mother allowed me to believe this, and you didn't dare question her. She was the disciplinarian in our home and if crossed, you were punished.

I suffered from her frequent bouts of physical and emotional abuse, which continued until the day I fought back. The last time my mother physically abused me, she snatched the poker from the fireplace, and chased me out of the house, swinging it back and forth like a broadsword, eventually striking my left side below the ribs with such force the metal poker bent. As I lay doubled over on the ground in the yard clutching my side, twisting and yelling out in pain, it occurred to her, perhaps she had gone too far this time. The tears she produced fell from her eyes as she begged for my forgiveness—and of course, I gave it. This display was common and if I didn't forgive my mother, she would give me the silent treatment and I found this tactic more painful than anything physical.

I was fourteen when the bodily harm toward me stopped, but the emotional abuse from her continued into adulthood and ultimately until the day she died.

Growing up, my sisters witnessed my parents' treatment toward me and replicated this learned behavior. I was ridiculed at home and at school by my two older sisters, who called me "Fagala" and made sure to inform all the kids on my first day of school I was a faggot. Early on, I didn't know what a faggot was, but coming from them it wasn't a good thing.

The inability to trust a sibling was also experienced by our queens. Joe grew up in Mount Vernon and lived near Reno's parents' home on Orchard Street. The boys went to the same school, ran in the same circles, and got into all kinds of trouble together. Though he was a typical American kid from a big Italian family, he was far from an average joe. He was a sensitive heartthrob, but he lacked confidence and didn't believe he was attractive.

Joe was a loner, at least that's what his friends thought. Only on certain occasions would he bring a friend home for his mother's Italian cooking, but even that stopped when he ran into his older sister when he was at the diner with Charlie. She cornered Joe later that day and teased him for hanging out with a queer. He could sense she was trying to get him to admit something and worried that she was beginning to figure out his secret. Only because her brother never went with girls, and he was too attractive not to be dating. Other than the time at the diner with Charlie, there was no way she could know, he was sure about that. Joe had no affectations like a lot of his friends, sometimes they could be too swishy. Joe wasn't that way, meaning, he didn't act like a girl. Joe felt he came across more like Reno and nobody could hide it better than Reno.

Dear Reno-

As you must know by know Joey
and I have not been seeing
much of each other, when we do
It's on the sneak, her sister,
and brother caught us at the Diner
one nite, and they both laid
Joe Out about being seen with
me, she told Joe to stay
away from me because I
look like a girl, and have a
bad reputation In mt Vernon.
there are going to be some
changes when you get back
nothing will be the same as
before with the gang.

Joe is always dishing
Mickey, and tells me she
does not want to be bothered
with her, but she is always
with her, they have been
getting very thick since
she is not seeing me.

OR until you answer
my letter I Remain

Your Friend
Always
Charlie

P.S.
Get busy with
the pen!
X + X +
X + X + +

Dear Reno,

As you must know by now Joe and I have not been seeing much of each other, when we do it's on the sneak, her sister, and brother caught us at the Diner one nite, and they both laid Joe out about being seen with me, she told Joe to stay away from me because I look like a girl, and have a bad reputation in Mount Vernon. There are going to be some changes when you get back nothing will be the same as before with the gang. Joe is always dishing Nickey, and tells me she does not want to be bothered with her, but she is always with her, they have been getting very thick since she is not seeing me. I really don't care because she can do as she pleases it really doesn't matter, I have found out a lot about Joe to know who she is.

Your friend always Charlie
P.S. Get busy with the pen. Xxxx xxxxxx

Homophobic laws at the time often left the queens exposed, revealing their deeper nature to their families. Daphne performed at the 82 on the weekends. She was relegated to the chorus and was presented as an exotic boy dancer to help with lifts and turns for the chorus girls. Daphne danced in the extravagant musical performances wearing beautifully designed costumes by Johnny Wong. Taking on different personas suited her and made perfect sense, she always felt as though she was born in the wrong family and often used her imagination to escape and "become" anyone other than herself. Some nights, she was a Spanish matador and other nights she would be a soldier in a show-stopping number. Daphne's theatrical ability to embody characters came easily to her. The pay wasn't much, but it was better than the alternative. Between her day job at the Department of Transportation and now this, it took pressure off her financially. She still had her regular john and if she played with trade, it was only with someone she knew.

Joe drove to Manhattan from Mount Vernon and was circling the block waiting for Daphne to come out of the 82 Club. She told Joe to meet her in front of the club. He was looking forward to hanging out with

Daphne; he hadn't seen her on the scene lately and couldn't wait to dish and share letters they had received from Reno. They had made plans earlier in the week to do the diner scene. It was the end of the month, which meant there was a good chance the underground gay clubs could be raided tonight. This was the reality when cops had quotas to meet. Relocating to a different venue was cool with Joe because Daphne was good at pulling in trade at the diner and Joe always benefited from what Daphne could "reel in" when they "went fishing."

Joe pulled slowly down the street as the performers came out of the 82 Club. Groups of men standing together on the sidewalk heckled the queens with homophobic and transphobic slurs, which was the norm. Unbothered, dressed as a boy, Daphne flew past the hecklers while waving at Joe as he pulled up. Joe leaned over and unlocked the door and Daphne slid into the front seat. The Mellow Tones were playing on the radio. Not wanting to be in full drag tonight, Daphne was feeling bummish; she applied just a touch of mascara and liner on her already pancaked face. Not too much, just enough to give a signal to a lucky fellow who may get an opportunity to be graced with Daphne's presence.

The diner was hopping! Cars were pulling up from both directions and the parking lot was packed. Luckily, Joe knew of a secret spot across the street near a quieter rural area. It was a smart spot to bring trade from the diner and mop in the back seat, as it was unlit and set back from the road. Teens and young adults were table hopping and laughter erupted from various groups as food and coffees were dropped off by waitresses in uniforms.

A group of nells giving fache with overly pancaked faces were sitting in a booth. A waitress delivered a tray of coffee cups filled with hot water to their table. One of the queens in the group reached for the ketchup and added it to a cup straight out of the bottle. With a spoon she stirred the concoction together to create a watered-down tomato soup, an economical meal when times were hard.

Joe recognized a couple of rubes he'd seen at the Bali a couple of weeks ago and he was determined he was going to mop on the blond number in the group. Charlie arrived on the scene in drag and was with a couple of chickens from her neighborhood. Seeing her walk into the diner, Joe abruptly excused himself to the tea room; he didn't want to deal with Charlie tonight. She's been "too much" lately, and it was clear to Daphne the two friends weren't getting along. Joe was right, Charlie was always the loudest queen in the room, no matter where she was; she was loud, "and she doesn't even have to open her mouth!"

Sept 14, 1957

Dear Reno.

Friday nite Daphny came up to mt News, looking for Chris we met him and made a Date for him to meet us he never showed up. The Diner is getting "Hotter" and Hotter by the minute, that nite their was four Detectives on foot patroling the Diner before they could question us we flew the coop, they took names and license plate numbers, the place was packed with Trade. So we rode around for awhile, and they we decided to go for a pie at Leri's you know the one on grandois Ave. There we met all the Trade

they came over to the table and
started to dish with me, they
wanted to know if we were
Roto-Rooters, meaning if we were
plumers you know what I mean, you
know the trade I am talking about.
Oh I almost forgot to tell you
they asked for you "Sorry". They
wanted to get Jone but we were
not to sure of them so we turned
them down all the I knew Half
of them and they know me. So
we left and drove Jaffney home
and Dished in front of her house
until four oclock in the A.M.
then Joe and I went home.
Well that's all the Dish for
now. I did not give peter
his picture yet, because he makes
dates and never keeps them. Oh
and another thing Ace keeps asking
for you, I'll give him your
love. You know the Dish Send
me one of your pictures of
the one in the Gold dress or the
one in the blonde wig. Goodbye
for now, Take care of yourself.
                Your Friend
                always
                Charlie

Hugs & Kisses
xxxx;
xxxx;

Sept 16, 1957

Dear Reno

Friday nite Daffney came to Mt Vernon, looking for Chris we met him and made a date for him to meet us he never showed up. The Diner is getting "hotter and hotter" by the minute, that nite their were four detectives on foot patrolling the Diner before they could question as we flew the coop, they took names and license plate numbers, the place was packed with trade. So we rode around for a while, and they we decided to go for a hot pie at Vera's you know the one on Gramatan Ave. There we met all the trade they came over to the table and started to dish with me, they wanted to know if we were Roto-Rooter's, meaning if we were plumbers you know what I mean, you know the trade I am talking about. Oh I almost forgot to tell you they asked for you. "Sorry." They wanted to get done but we were not to sure of them so we turned them down all tho I know half of them and they know me. So we left and drove Daffney home and dished in front of her house until 4 o'clock in the a.m. Then Joe and I went home. Well that's all the dish for now. I did not give Peter your picture yet, because he makes dates and never keeps them. Oh and another thing Ace keeps asking for you, I'll give him your love.

"You know the dish." Send me one of your pictures of the one in the gold dress or the one in the blond wig. Goodbye for now, take care of yourself.

Your Friend Always Charlie

Love and kisses xxxxx

Daphne was standing by the jukebox when the cops strolled in. The energy and the volume of noise in the place dimmed a little, as they passed each table and scrutinized the patrons. Daphne looked away from the cops; she could feel her heart beating in her chest as panic set in. She decided the best course of action was to step outside without being noticed by the cops who were coming right toward her. Her head down, she stepped past the officers and

headed to the exit. Just as she put her hand on the swinging door one of the cops grabbed her by the shoulder and spun her around, bringing Daphne face to face with him. With no words, he shook his head, as if in disgust, slapped a cuff on her wrist and led her outside. Joe was coming out of the bathroom and stopped when he saw the cops detaining Daphne. She had been wearing too much makeup for plausible deniability, and as Charlie was in full drag, she was pinched too.

Well so far the Diner is still jumps but the cops are always telling us to get the hell out of there and stay away, Joe and I were stopped by the cops Thursday nite at 1:30 in the morning.

Daphne, Charlie and four boys in makeup were arrested, hauled to jail, and booked on masquerading charges. That night, as Daphne sat in a cell with the other queens from the diner, she thought of her older sister, whom she looked up to, and remembered the time she caught her trying on one of her party dresses.

Michael had been a boy of about five. "You look very pretty, Micky." She remembered her warning, "Don't let Papa see you dressed like that. Don't let Papa see you."

Daphne felt nauseous recalling this and knew it was a matter of time now before Papa would know the big secret. Wallowing in her anguish, Daphne kept her head down and stared at the floor. Suddenly she recognized her father's thick Italian accent echoing off the walls in the corridor outside the cell. She looked up through the bars as he approached.

"That's him. That's my boy." Seeing the look on her father's face sickened her. Mr. Alogna's pained expression was obvious as he stood next to the police officer, holding his hat in front of him with both hands.

"Michael Alogna," the guard called out. Daphne stepped forward as the iron bars slid to the side.

Mr. Alogna couldn't look his son in the eyes. Every parent's nightmare is hearing the phone ring in the middle of the night with a police officer on the other end. One of his own children had been arrested and if that wasn't bad enough, seeing Michael now with these people was agony.

"Papa," Daphne said quietly.

"What are you doing here, Micky?" he asked, defeated. Daphne could hear the confusion in his father's voice. "What are you doing here with all these Suzies?" he questioned. "Suzie" was the name his Italian father gave to queer people.

Daphne could feel a lump in in her belly. "I'm sorry, Papa," was all she could muster.

Mr. Alogna didn't say another word until they stepped outside the police station. The sunlight was bright, and Daphne couldn't hide the fact she was still wearing traces of makeup.

On the sidewalk away from the cops and displaying less control, Mr. Alogna demanded, "Wipe that shit off your face," handing his son his handkerchief. He continued, "Why do you look like a Suzie?"

Daphne attempted to rub the makeup off her face, "I'm sorry, Papa," she repeated.

The realization was overwhelming to Mr. Alogna. "I didn't know you were a Suzie," he said, with disgust.

Hearing that word come from her father's mouth, directed at her, cut like a knife. Daphne noticed a big husky driver getting out of a delivery truck nearby. "Papa, you see that man? He could be a Suzie," she pointed out.

"What are you talking about? He's a man."

She could feel her father's agitation. Daphne kept going, "He could be a Suzie, Papa—not all Suzies look like a Suzie."

Her father's agitation turned to anger as the lid flew off the pot; Mr. Alogna had reached his boiling point, "Then why don't you look like a man? If you're going to be a Suzie—don't let the sins in your heart show on your face."

And as Daphne's father struggled in disbelief, he turned to his son and made himself clear, "Don't wear the shit!"

Mr. Alogna never spoke to his son regarding his sexuality again. After that day was behind him, he carried on as though the conversation had never taken place.

Daphne's Hungarian-born mother had a different take on finding out her son was a homosexual. They say "a mother is the first to know and the last to find out" their child is gay. Early on, she knew her son was different, but none of that mattered. To her, he was a gift. Of course, she worried about the dangers this existence could be for her son, but she worried about all her children. She loved him and took it upon herself to be his strongest ally. He was his mother's best friend, and she supported him until her death, challenging the rigid and homophobic social codes of the 1950s and onwards by offering her son unconditional love and radical acceptance.

CHAPTER NINE

Lalo

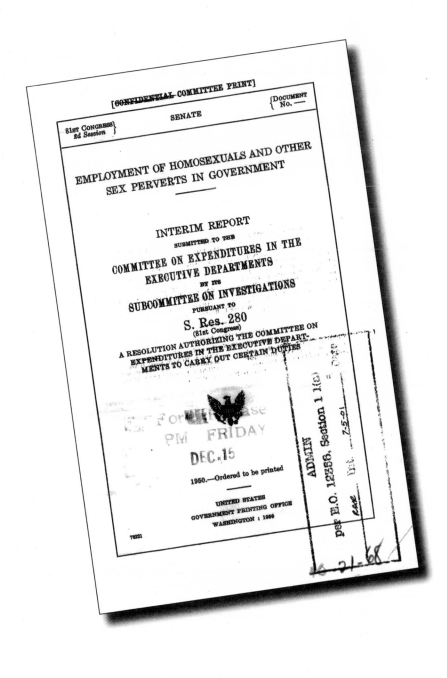

[CONFIDENTIAL COMMITTEE PRINT]

{DOCUMENT No. ——

SENATE

81st Congress }
2d Session }

EMPLOYMENT OF HOMOSEXUALS AND OTHER SEX PERVERTS IN GOVERNMENT

INTERIM REPORT

SUBMITTED TO THE

COMMITTEE ON EXPENDITURES IN THE EXECUTIVE DEPARTMENTS

BY ITS

SUBCOMMITTEE ON INVESTIGATIONS

PURSUANT TO

S. Res. 280
(81st Congress)

A RESOLUTION AUTHORIZING THE COMMITTEE ON EXPENDITURES IN THE EXECUTIVE DEPARTMENTS TO CARRY OUT CERTAIN DUTIES

1950.—Ordered to be printed

UNITED STATES
GOVERNMENT PRINTING OFFICE
WASHINGTON : 1950

76221

oming out or it being discovered you were gay in America during the 1950s was extremely difficult. This was a time when no lawyer would represent a known homosexual. LGBTQ+ men and women had no civil rights and police involvement on any level was hard to avoid because of the laws that were put in place by the government. This is a major factor when understanding the stigmatization of the gay community. The desire to propagate fear of "the other" in the populous has always been an agenda, a campaign to push fear into suburban communities and into people's homes. People fear what they don't understand, and without proper education or compassion, marginalized people prove to be the perfect scapegoat. Their difference can be exploited, presented as a threat to traditional values and morality. Simply put: to keep the population in line, keep them ignorant. This systemic discrimination has historically been employed against anyone who isn't a white, Christian cisgender man: whether that be due to sex, economic status, disability, or race.

This idea is still in play today in the twenty-first century. Forward-thinking people who seek information and enact change know that education is the key to understanding. Thankfully we have evolved as a society and grown through technology and science, and information is more accessible than ever before. We can also thank advocates and agencies in our communities, who have fought for years for LGBTQ+ people to have equal rights. Sadly, the push, now, is to protect the rights our communities have fought so hard to acquire. There are certain groups who will always fight just as hard *against* equality for all Americans because of homophobia, bigotry, misogyny, and racism. We can also expect resistance from people who simply don't want to learn about marginalized groups, because in their world none of this affects them. Or does it?

American post-war society was about conformity. Traditional, binary roles of men and women were put in place by conservative society, and one followed the rule of law and order. After being enlisted into the military, many young American men left their small towns to fight in the Second World War. These soldiers, many of whom had never left the state they were born in, suddenly found themselves thrust into an unfamiliar world. Within the confines of the military, they depended solely on their own sex for survival and companionship, which ultimately resulted in a camaraderie between likeminded men. Women were simultaneously leaving the home, taking jobs to replace the men for the war effort.

After the Second World War many soldiers had seen the world and experienced a different way of life. Women were making contributions to society outside their domestic roles in the home. They didn't want to go back to the kitchen and many men didn't want to return to suburban life. The U.S. government took note that there was a rebellion towards returning to pre-war Law and Order. post-war America was the age of the "great gay migration." White gay men and women diverged from white suburbanization, and it was realized they weren't reproducing—which, by all accounts of the period, was the American ideal.

The U.S. government began to understand many of these people were flocking to the big cities and settling in neighborhoods that catered to specific communities. Campaigns to prevent this were carried out on local, state and federal levels, which included FBI involvement. Political bureaucrats started seeking ways to suppress and confine people not living by the values and ideals put in place by white conservatives. If you were anything other than what is considered "normal" you were a criminal or labeled a communist. Gays and lesbians were treated as violators of local, state and federal laws.

The Red Scare coincided with the Lavender Scare. While both acts were initially aimed at hunting down, identifying and removing "undesirable" employees from federal agencies, the brushfire of panic quickly spread to the entertainment community and ultimately to everyday life. Any American perceived to be a Communist sympathizer during the Red Scare trials would be interrogated and, if found guilty, punished by immediate loss of employment and being placed on the infamous "black ball" list. The Lavender Scare was created to root out those suspected of being homosexual or engaging in any form of queer expression. Amid the groundswell of post-Second World-War social conservatism, queer people were undoubtedly a threat to the traditional mid-twentieth-century American nuclear family ideals. This omnipresent persecution and intolerance gave rise to the widely used phrase "The Homosexual Menace."

If all that wasn't enough, drag queens were continually at risk of being arrested by way of the very antiquated but repurposed New York State Masquerade Law, as previously mentioned. Originally enforced in the mid-nineteenth century, the Masquerade Law prohibited alteration of one's face through makeup or paint to disguise one's identity on a public road or setting. Apparently, at that time, it wasn't unusual for a rural farmer to appropriate the outward appearance of a Native American field worker to evade tax collectors. It was based on this law that police were able to arrest those who were dressing outside of their traditional regimented gender roles, aka drag. During the 1950s the Masquerade Law was increasingly put into service around the country to punish gender variance and used as a campaign to discriminate against homosexuals. There was a "three-garment" rule that gender non-conforming homosexuals understood and passed on to each other. Individuals must have three articles of clothing on their person aligning with their born gender identity. This wasn't enshrined in law, but the lore on the streets suggesting this was a way to avoid a jail sentence.

The U.S. Congress issued a report titled "Employment of Homosexuals and Other Sex Perverts in Government." It concluded that homosexuality was a mental illness and that homosexuals constituted "security risks to the nation," as they were more susceptible to blackmail. As such, they were labeled un-American. Police harassment escalated in cities and neighborhoods as a response. Oppression and punishment came in the form of entrapment. The FBI and law enforcement agencies inserted themselves into the gay subculture in order to police sexual and gender deviance.

Plainclothes policemen would frequent known queer spaces, including bars, restaurants and cruising spots, allowing themselves to be approached by gay men. If an individual struck up a conversation with an undercover officer, they were arrested for "soliciting" sex, as the act of cruising was deemed a criminal act that fell into the broader category of "disorderly conduct." Not only would the individual be incarcerated, but the bar itself would then be fined and/or closed for being disorderly.

This was a very real concern to the letter writers, and indeed many of them suffered at the hands of the laws around disorderly conduct. One such person was Ed Limato.

Confidence was Ed's strongest trait, followed by a wicked sense of humor inherited from his mother, Angelina. Angelina was another tough Italian mama. Like Joe's mom, she would do anything for her son. Ed could do no wrong in his mother's eyes; Angelina was a girl in a house full of boys and tossed disciplining out the window when he, the last of her three sons, entered the world. Ed had two older brothers and he was the baby. He was raised to respect his parents and he did when he was at home. However, out on the streets he was a wildcat.

Ed kept secrets and in his teens joined a gang in his Italian neighborhood, with leather jacket and all. The Fulton Dukes were a bunch of self-proclaimed bad boys who would cruise the streets and alleys harassing girls while looking to see what rivals they could jump. But if Angelina had discovered Ed's *other* secret, it would surely have killed her: Ed liked boys. He hid behind a masculine bad boy façade. This edgy image made him popular with girls and some buddies his age. Ed didn't believe he was a queer because he didn't act or sound like the obvious ones his gang would terrorize around town. If the other members knew how bad he felt for the queer kids his gang tormented, they would think he was a fairy too.

Secretly, Ed idolized actresses from the silver screen. He loved going to the movies and every week he would take a couple of quarters from Angelina's purse for a Saturday matinee. (He snuck into the theater and kept the quarters.) There was something about seeing movie stars come alive on the big screen that appealed to young Ed. He was fascinated by glamorous stars and the costumes they wore. In fact, he dreamt of going to Hollywood someday. It was nice to dream, but he knew he had to get out into the world as there was a lot to discover—he was sure of that.

He found himself taking rides into the city in his friend Joe's new car. The two boys frequented clubs in New York looking to hook up with girls. But ultimately at the end of the night they discovered they didn't need them. Somehow alcohol was the excuse for hooking up with your buddy if you struck out with the girls. Which could happen and did, on more than one occasion, in Joe's car. Ed began to run around the streets of New York and met an entirely new group of friends who appealed to him more than the ones in his suburban town of Mount Vernon. He made friends easily in this new arena, because he was good-looking and offered a good time. He introduced himself to this new group as Reno Martin. Hanging out in Greenwich Village he met up with the likes of Daphne, Josephine, and their merry band of misfits. It wasn't long before Reno was introduced to the underworld of drag. His newfound friends intrigued him because they were different and one thing Reno loved most was to surround himself with people that were really "out there."

Reno was driven. As much as he was having fun on the streets, his aspirations of wanting more out of life took hold, and he enrolled himself in broadcasting courses and applied himself to become a radio disk jockey. This was exciting for him because he was taking his first step towards his dream. This new venture took him to Louisiana, where he landed a job at a local radio station in New Orleans as a radio announcer.

Reno was in his early twenties when he stepped off the bus in New Orleans. It was the first time in his young life he had no one to lean on and for someone who came from a big family, whose mother prepared every meal and had friends he could see daily, being alone was a rude awakening. When Reno wasn't working at the station, he would walk the streets of the Old Quarter and eventually found places to frequent and meet trade.

Reno took a shine to a handsome local boy, who happened to be Black. Unlike so many others, color was never an issue for Reno. The boy asked Reno out for coffee and picked him up in his car in front of his apartment. Later that same evening when being dropped off, Reno leaned in to give his new friend a kiss that began to turn passionate. They were interrupted by a tap on the window of the car. A policeman who witnessed these two men locked in an embrace arrested them both and Reno went to state prison.

Angelina would take a bus from New York to New Orleans every month to bring a care package and visit her incarcerated son. Reno lost his job at the radio station, of course. Not wanting to return to his old life in New York, despite his mother's pleading, he stayed in New Orleans and got a job at the Club My-O-My, a sleazy female impersonation club located over the water at the Lakefront.

It is hard to imagine that what little Reno was doing in the car with his Black friend was highly indecent and punishable by law. Sexual behavior was a risk between biracial heterosexual and homo-sexuals couples and if caught you were certain to get jail time.

Dear Reno.

I really don't Care because
she can do as she pleases It
really doesn't matter, I have
found out a lot about joe to
Know how she is.
I have been getting Into
some fights about you,
~~some queens from~~
New Rochelle have been
dishing you very evil to
~~Jerrde up~~ at the diner
and a few other places
In mt Vernon, I. smacked
one of the queens already
from mamaraneck.
Oh here is another dish that
has been going around about
you, Richard the ~~Canard~~ has
been telling all the Trade
that you are a dish Jockey,
and not working In drag
of course I tell them
Richard is a lier, and that
you are working at the
~~mtomy~~ club In drag
why have you not been
Writing to me lately,
Are you still bugged with

me, about not coming out.
Send let me know if
you plain to stay out
there for a while, I don't
know your plains wether
your coming home soon
or not, ooo please write
and let me know if I
should come out or not.
Well Rose I can't think
of any thing more to
say so until my next
letter.
OR until you answer
my letter I Remain

Your friend
always.
Charlie

P.S.
Get busy with
the pen.
I + I
I + I + I

Dear Reno

I have been getting into some fights about you, some queens from New Rochelle have been dishing you very evil to trade up at the diner and a few other places in Mount Vernon, I smacked one of the queens already.

Oh here is another dish that has been going around about you, Richard the Anaid has been telling all the trades that you are a disc jockey, and not working in drag of course I tell them Richard is a lier, and that you were working at the "my-o-my" club in drag.

Why have you not been writing to me lately, are you still bugged with me, about not coming out. Reno let me know if you plain to stay out there for a while, I don't know your plains wether you're coming home soon or not, so please write and let me know if I should come out or not. Well Rose I can't think of anything more to say so until my next letter.

Or until you answer my letter I remain.

Your friend
Charlie

Establishments could be shut down for serving alcohol to a queer person under the law, too. Police raids were commonplace and always expected.

February 23-1958

Dear Reno:

Hope everything is OK with you.
I am fine and hope you are too. I haven't
written you much lately because I've been
in so much I just didn't have anything
to dish about, but I went out this weekend so now I have a little dishing.

Friday night I met Charlie around
the Tavir and she said Richard would
be there at 10:30 and they were going downtown, anyway we never did go, so I went
home early. Saturday night I decided
to go Downtown, so I went to the Cork
It's very hot, many cops, they didn't
even want to let me in, finally Tere
got me in, Micky, Jimmy and Johnny
O'Connor and some other number were there
I was dishing with them, they all asked
for you, later Igere came in, she
had to go through the same thing I had
to get in, we left after a while and
went over to the 41 g, from there to
the Waldorf, Hopkins was there, Richard
S, Joe Charles Camp ey and some other
number. Richard is trying for scene with a
next number. New York is very hot
cops all over, they even come into the
Waldorf and Cheek, hardly no queens paint
they have to be very careful.

Yours
Joe.

February 23, 1958

Dear Reno:

Hope everything is OK with you. I am fine and hope you are too. I haven't written you much lately because I've been in so much I just didn't have anything to dish about, but I went out this weekend so now I have a little dishing.

Friday night I met Charlie around the Diner and she said Richard would be there at 10:30 and they were going Downtown, anyway we never did go, so I went home early. Saturday night I decided to go Downtown, so I went to the Cork. Its very hot, many cops, they didn't even want to let me in, finally Tere got me in, Micky, Jimmy, and Johnny O'Connor and some other number were there. I was dishing with them, they all asked for you, later Daphne came in, she had to go through the some thing I had to get in, we left after a while and went over to the 415, from there to the Waldorf, Josephine was there, Richard L., Joe, Charlie's camp ex, and some other number. New York is very hot.

Cops all over, they even came into the Waldorf and Chick, hardly no queens paint they have to be careful.

Yours Joe

Some bars provided dancing in the basement, usually filled with queer men and women. A large, bare red light bulb was often affixed to the wall next to the entry door. When a raid commenced on the main floor the light bulb would blink and the dancing patrons would quickly swap partners. By the time the cops entered, all they found were men dancing with women thereby avoiding any arrests. If caught on the streets or in a private residence dressed as the opposite sex you were stopped, harassed, and most likely arrested by the police, also known as "the Vice." The worst time for a drag queen was walking on the streets or in public spaces. If clocked, they would spend five months to a year in jail and risk physical violence or death from local citizens as well as police officers.

You know the cork is quite the scene for pan caked faces again. Even Algene goes there now. She's going with Jerry Brown's ex husband. He's a doll. I used to go to High School with him. Jerry's in jail for four months. She was caught in drag at the Wagon Wheel. Her friend Shelly, was working there in drag as the hat check girl. She's that pale redhead. Remember her? She's always in the can too. The cops had known Jerry. She was sitting at a table with Shelly when the bulls pinched her! They never knew her girlfriend was a fraud too! Poor Jerry. She'll be out in the spring.

I met Burma on the train the other day. She goes to the Cork too. Along with Marty. So does Amber. Now that my hair is long + my eyes on a Burmish kick, I'm in the mood to paint like crazy + make an appearance there tommorow night. Carmen + Hazel were there last week too. I saw Joe & Charlie in the Waldorf Saturday. Richie arnaud was there too. With some beauties. Camille's roomate Carla mopped on one.

Marilyn (the real one) was walking in front of Camille's place where she works yesterday. Camille said she looked the end fatch. No makeup, no stockings, straw hair and a mink coat. She had the coat tightly wrapped around her famous ass, and was shaking it like mad! Marilyn (from Brooklyn) would have died to be there! Incidently I heard she moved out on Kira. And guess where to? — So. Offord St. I heard "Fran" babe was there already telling her "Now Tony jeweler — no trade, I'll get your lamps, and — etc. etc." "It seems to me I've heard this song before." History repeats itself. I havn't seen hide or hair of the wolf girl Georgie.

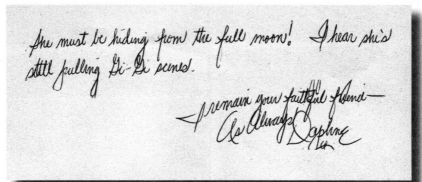

She must be hiding from the full moon! I hear she's still pulling Bi-Bi scenes.

I remain your faithful friend— As Always Daphne

from letter dated February 7, 1958

Dear Reno

You know the Cork is quite the scene for pancaked faces lately. Even Algene goes there now. She's going with Jerry Brown's ex husband. He's a doll. I used to go to high school with him. Jerry's in jail for four months. She was caught in drag at the Wagon Wheel. Her friend Shelly, was working there in drag as the hat check girl. She's that pale redhead. Remember her? She's always in the can too. The cops had known Jerry. She was sitting at a table with Shelly when the balls pinched her! They never knew her girlfriend was a fraud too! Poor Jerry. She'll be out in the Spring.

As Always—Daphne

At the shameful epicentre stood the infamous Women's House of Detention in the West Village, just a block from The Stonewall Inn, which housed women who were incarcerated for stepping outside their assigned gender role in dress or mannerisms. Ironically, this prison galvanized the flourishing lesbian community in Greenwich Village during the 1950s. Once women were released from the House of D, they found community in the Greenwich Village neighborhood; a bond had formed from serving time together. Some wanted to remain close by to frequently visit those still imprisoned.

The people who sought to punish these women for daring to be themselves had inadvertently and unwittingly helped create and fortify the queer community they sought to abolish. Social activism and gay liberation began to ignite in cities and universities even before the Stonewall uprising. The Matachin Society, formed by activist Harry Hay in the 1950s, is one of the first gay rights groups in the United States which supported homosexuals and social acceptance. In turn, the Daughters of Bilitis was the first lesbian rights organization founded in the mid-1950s by Phyllis Lyon and Del Martin.

Queer people walked with several well-defined targets on their back. This fact makes the misadventures of the queens in these letters even more remarkable. An innocent stroll to the corner market for a quart of milk had the very real potential for a disastrous outcome. Living as an outsider, rebel or renegade has always come at personal cost, and our queens were certainly no exception to that inescapable reality. The letters and their writers share no exception to run-ins with the Law. Often the writers themselves exposed their own criminal behavior and punishment when dishing with Reno. Of course, it isn't surprising the Boomatzas would eventually be involved in an FBI investigation.

CHAPTER TEN

Crime

Dear René;

well the latest scene was that Claudia and I mopped at the Met (35) pastons all gorgeous White Red, Brown, Black, every color you can think of the end wigs. there's a white one thats like for you Ponga Ponga white hair like this paper down to the ass. (Pity)!!!!!! next, most of them flew already for 75 & 50 I have a Blonde Paste-on all around Pony tail thats Fab! be mopped ___ Speaking of mopping I just left Daphne I got shoes & gold coin $35.00 She bought Black fruit toots, She might go drags whith the white wig & white sheath & white Foxes. They're all going Mascair, Sal everyone's going ___ (can you make it) I'll hold on to a (white) one for you !!

Short Hair

well I'm going to bed now ___→
so write soon ___ I Called Billy Baker she was suprised you hav'nt written her. She's making my Silver Bugle Beaded Sheathh for Phils.
              Goodnite
(P.S.
(Burin this)
letter
Please ((that met scene was in the Papers) (don't dich)
          Josphine Bzks ___ ↓

Dear René:

Well, the latest scene was that Claudia and I mopped at the Met (35) pastons all gorgeous white, red, brown, black, every color, you can think of the end wigs. There's a white one that's like for your Ponga Ponga white hair like this paper down to the ass (pity)!!!!! Next most of them flew already for $75 and $50. I have a Blonde paste-on all around ponytail that's fab! We mopped speaking of mopping I just left Daphne I got shoes and gold coin $35. She bought black fur boots. She might go dragg with the white wig and white sheath and white foxes. They're all going Mascani, Sal everyone's going (can you make it). I'll hold on to a white one for you!!

Well I'm going to bed now so write soon I called Billy Baker she was surprised you haven't written her. She's making my silver bugle beaded sheath for Phils.

Goodnite

Josephine Baker

(P.S. BURN this letter please.)

(That met scene was in the papers.) (Don't dish.)

Josephine and Claudia broke in and stole a collection of wigs from an institution that represented the bastion of class, taste, and glamor: the Metropolitan Opera House in New York. But what began as a dare morphed into something far larger. It was explained by Diaz many years later how the wig caper went down—insisting the newspaper article had gotten it wrong. He was adamant, "They did not get in with the dancers!" as explained in the papers.

It was Saturday afternoon and Claudia and Josephine strolled past the Metropolitan Opera House. Josephine noticed that one of the arched gated entrances, primarily for bringing in props and sets, had been accidentally left unlocked. Not missing an opportunity, they slipped in. It was opportunism at its finest—not the meticulously planned crime that one might imagine. As fate would have it, the Met was empty that day and as they entered the hallowed halls of the opera house, Josephine and Claudia quietly made their way up a staircase and found themselves on stage.

Claudia remembers fondly how she looked out into the darkness of an empty theater and was struck by the beauty of the chandelier hanging high above the audience. Center stage, she dropped to her knees. "I got my cookies off. I did," she proudly recalls.

Josephine, witnessing this act, whispered loudly, "What are you doing?!"

Claudia's reply: "I'm saving a memory, that's what I am doing!"

The two slowly ascended a circular staircase to the fourth floor and noticed a door labeled WIG ROOM. *That's all any queen needs to see!* The pair went into action and kicked the door in, breaking the lock. Inside, they were stunned by the vast treasure of tresses they had uncovered. The finest imported human hair wigs of every major opera from *Carmen* to *Tosca* were all meticulously displayed. Without a moment to waste, Josephine and Claudia made quick work of snatching every wig in sight. Grabbing large trash bags, they stuffed the wigs inside and made their way out the same way they entered. Once back out on the street they ran for it, all the way back to the trick room.

The following Monday, Nina, the head wig costumer at the Met, opened the door to the wig room, only to find bald wig stands bearing silent witness to the theft. You can imagine her shock and horror. Meanwhile, Josephine and Claudia were being entrepreneurial with their haul of illicit stash. They were busy selling off the bulk of their haul to the 82 Club and Moroccan Village Show Queens. They pawned the wigs for $50–$75, a hefty sum for that time. Although they were easily worth six times that much, the promise of easy cash in such abundance was too appealing to Josephine and Claudia, who had likely never seen this much money. And at those prices they flew. It was a deal most queens couldn't refuse!

STRANGE OPERA WIG THEFTS SOLVED WITH ARREST OF TWO

NEW YORK ⑰ — The strange theft case at the Met has been solved. Police arrested two men on charges of stealing 33 wigs.

Disappearance of the false hair-pieces from a fifth-floor costume room of the Metropolitan Opera House had been under investigation for two months. They were valued at $3,000.

Detectives accused Robert Perez, 23, a hairdresser, and Claudio Siaz, 22, a waiter, of taking the wigs, and selling them.

Nine young men also were seized and charged with possession of stolen property. Others are being sought. Seventeen of the wigs have been recovered.

Well here's Hedda again giving you the latest dish! This lady is a tramp, but unlike the song, she does dish the dirt with the rest of the girls. So Jayne found romance in Alexandria eh? It sounds like the end scene my dear but take some advice from your love-wise sister and stay up on your toes. Play it cool and you won't get kicked where it hurts most. If I know you, by the time you read this, the whole affair will most likely be a thing of the past. I hope not, but if so just mark it down as another exiting chapter in the life of Renay Adora - belle of New Orleans! Things are looking pretty Kammish for me too lately. The rubiest thing here right now is the weather. There's much snow on the ground now, and its hailing and raining. But I have that "who cares" attitude right now. A feeling I haven't had in quite a while. For a change there have been quite a few brainny developments in these parts.

Claudia's back in town. She was in Florida you know. She's back on the scene with Josphine. I saw them both at the Cork. (I heard they have intentions of going to the Madi Gras) They camped four paste-ons from the Metropolitan Opera House. They sold one to Terry, one to Ruby from Bklyn, and kept the other two. I heard that Johnny De Blanco is holding his Madi-Gras drag at the Chateau Garden on the 14th. I'm dying to go. Josie said she'd lend me the red wig + douch it on me. However, I have to git it straight with her tonight or tomorow of I see her at the Cork. When is the Madi Gras in New Orleans?

I remain your faithful friend —

As Always, Daphine

from letter dated February 7, 1958

Claudia's back in town. She was in Florida you know. She's back on the scene with Josephine. I saw them both at the Cork. (I heard they have intentions of going to the Mardi Gras). They camped four paste-ons from the Metropolitan Opera House. They sold one to Terry, one to Ricky from Bklyn, and kept the other two. I heard that Johnny De Franco is holding his Mardi Gras drag at the Chateau Garden on the 14th. I'm dying to go. Josie said she'd lend me the red wig + douch it on me. However I have to get it straight with her tonight or tomorrow if I see her at the Cork. When is the Mardi Gras in New Orleans?

I remain, As Always (your faithful friend)

Daphne

Just about every Show Queen bought at least one wig as the deal was too good to pass up. There was, however, a major glitch in the scheme they hadn't accounted for: an ex-Show Queen, who had left the 82 Club to pursue full time employment in the Theatrical Wardrobe Union, coincidentally worked at the Metropolitan Opera House; none other than the former *Salome* headliner Henry "Adrian" Arango, who performed "Dance of the Seven Veils."

Adrian also showed up for work on Monday and learning that thousands of dollars' worth of lace front handmade human hair wigs had been stolen, suggested the wigs may have been purchased by female impersonators. The news of the theft hit the papers and justice was to be served. The police notified the FBI, who questioned everyone. Soon, the FBI raided the dressing room at Club 82 with Adrian and Nina in tow.

Immediately, Nina pointed out several wigs which sat on the heads of their new owners and were quickly snatched off by the authorities. As much as the queens appealed to the FBI—as far as they knew they had bought them fairly—all who were wearing the wigs were immediately rounded up and arrested for possession of stolen goods. They all served time.

Ultimately, Claudia and Josephine returned the rest of the stolen wigs to the authorities. Or so the FBI thought. Ingeniously, the duo swapped out the beautiful, handmade coiffures for cheap synthetic wigs. They figured the cops wouldn't know the difference—and they were right! As they say, crime doesn't pay, and in Josephine and Claudia's case it surely didn't—well, not at those rock bottom prices. Both were arrested for trespassing, and both spent a year in jail at Ryker's Island Penitentiary.

When recounting this story several years later, Claudia Diaz opened a small bag. Inside was a sixty-five-year-old lace front wig that she had kept in secret as a souvenir. She defiantly added, "Fuck you, NYPD! Two faggots from Brooklyn outsmarted the whole lot of you—and you still don't know how we got in!"

CHAPTER ELEVEN

Surviving

he letters in this book, and numerous others that haven't been included, serve as snapshots of the experiences of young, queer people in the 1950s. Their stories resonated with me to such an extent that I, alongside many friends and experts, have spent years piecing their lives together, to better understand who they were, where they came from and where their lives led.

We found Daphne first, then Claudia. And others, like Terry Noel and Adrian, all of whom bravely shared their stories. Of course, it all started with my friend Ed Limato, otherwise known as Reno Martin. He was the central point from which I was able to establish contact with these incredible people; he set me on this journey.

This book explores the highs and lows of the Boomatzas, and the wider group of queer people living and working in New York in the 1950s. There are many more voices we will never hear, who also had dreams and anxieties, interior lives and fears about the future. I was lucky enough to get know the letter writers on the page. But the reality of their lives, which were hard and fast, glittering but on the fringes of society, meant that this story is not an altogether happy one. The world did not protect them—they protected one another, but for some of them it wasn't enough. They did not all reach a happy, safe adulthood. They did not all see the ways in which the world has become more accepting of people like them. That's the reality of sharing their words, and it would be misleading to pretend otherwise.

November 17, 1958

Dear Reno:

Well how are things with you, I am fine and hope to hear the same from you.

Well this has been a very dead week, and an even more dead weekend. no popping, so I can't dish anything about that dept.

Some time ago my brother-in-law the Cop, saw me with Charlie and Ray in front of Charlies house, I don't know if he got a good look at Charlie but anyway I chatted with him for a few minutes and then I left.

Yesterday my brother told me that Gary the Cop told him he didn't like the people I was hanging around with I don't know if he asked him the queen scene or not so I'll have to be extra careful about hanging around in Mt. Vernon. Anyway Reno. from now on send your letters to my Job. c/o Gramco Printers, 27 Milburn Street. Bronxville, N. Y. just in case.

I spent a boring Friday night in Yonkers and went downtown with Chickie. Saturday Night we went with Richard S., Tommie and that Blonde Mickey the one I met with you in New Rochelle one night Tennie the John mopped on (one) him, the rest of us left and came home. Have you heard that Stonewalk is closed? That Richard let nutty Tommie drive home from New York, he scared the shit out of Chickie and myself I don't know

why Richie lets him Augie, and if he
keeps it up I don't think he'll have that
station wagon for long.
Charlie would like to know why
you don't write her, and you were
right about that call I should have called
Station to Station & the next time I
call, I'll do that, not much more to dish
so I'll close, be good,

That address is
c/o Gramco Printers
27 MILBURN ST.
Bronxville, N.Y.

Your Friend
Joe.

November 17, 1958

Dear Reno:

Well, how are things with you? I am fine and hope to hear the
same from you.

Well, this has been a very dead week, and an even more dead
weekend, no mopping, so I can't dish anything about that dept.

Some time ago my brother-in-law the cop, saw me with Charlie
and Raj in front of Charlie's house, I don't know if he got a good
look at Charlie but anyway, I dished with him for a few minutes
and then I left. Yesterday my brother told me that Gary the cop
told him he didn't like the people I was hanging around with I
don't know if he dished him the queen scene or not, so I'll have
to be extra careful about hanging around in Mt. Vernon. Anyway,
Reno from now on send your letters to my job, c/o Gramco
Printers, 27 Milburn Street, Bronxville, N.Y. just in case.

Your Friend, Joe

Claudia (born Claudio) Diaz's journey had taken her down dark paths while seeking kindness and acceptance from others. Claudio was a part of a broken system. The institutions of family, law enforcement, social justice and pastoral care all failed him repeatedly. Without the correct guidance, he was placed in juvenile detention centers, sent to a psychiatric hospital, and ultimately turned out and left to fend for himself as a teenager on the streets of New York City. With no biological family support of his own, his friends were his chosen family: Josephine, Daphne, Billie, Charlie and GiGi. They were as supportive as young people could be, but they all had their own issues of adversity. Claudio knew when it came right down to it, he was faced with a sobering realization. He had to take care of himself to survive. He had to make a choice. "Do you want to live, or do you want to die?" was a question he asked himself often.

Claudio spent a year at Ryker's Island penitentiary with Roberto for his role in the wig heist and admits it was the hardest year of his life. He refused to discuss the horrors of this time with me. However, Claudio did survive that period of his life and it was because of the love of his friends. Had it not been for meeting Josephine at the Cork Club so many years ago, he couldn't imagine what would have happened to him. Despite everything, he survived them all.

Hi There!

Sorry I couldnt write sooner, heres hoping to find you in good spirits.

Well The beach is marvelous to say the least The weather is fantastic every night so far in the 80's — very romantic. as far as trade is concerned well, you must know by now if you have money & lots of it you can get Lana Turner numbers, but there are always a few floaters here & there to be mopped on, they are all hustlers the majority — many many blonde beauties on the beach, many garbones also.

as far as having a ball down here theres a million places to go to the bars close at 5. pm + then there are the after hour joints. many besies town here. Its like an elegant Atlantic City, only much cleaner + prettier sights to see theres much loot to be made down here if your a call girl, but I'm afraid I threw in the high heels for a while. Theres a lovely queen here, shes a beauty, Johny bays face + Steve Reeves body. very sweet she works at the Onyx Club in drag - very yummy you should see her you'll crack. Well keewee I'll have to close for now I'll write you soon.
- Regards —> Josephine

Hi there!

Sorry I couldn't write sooner, here's hoping to find you in good spirits. Well the beach is marvelous to say the least. The weather is fantastic every night so far in the 80s very romantic. As far as trade is concerned well, you must know by now if you have money and lots of it you can get Lana Turner numbers but there are always a few floaters here and there to be mopped on, they are all hustlers the majority many many blonde beauties on the beach, many gaberones also.

As for having a ball down here and there's a million places to go to the bars close at 5 AM + then there are the after hour joints, many lesies down here. It's like an elegant Atlantic City, only much cleaner and prettier sights to see, there's much loot to be made down here if your a call girl, but I'm afraid I threw in the high heels for a while, there's a lovely queen here, she's a beauty, Johnny boy's face + Steve Reeves body, very sweet she works at the Onyx Club in dragg very rummy you should see her, you'll crack. Well Renee I'll have to close for now I'll write you soon.

Regards, Josephine

Roberto "Josephine" Perez, died of AIDS. Her mother, having never fully accepted her son for being gay, blamed her queer friends for her death. She never wanted to see any of them ever again and refused to allow them to attend her funeral, turning them away at the church. Not even Claudia, Josephine's best friend whom she had known since she was a boy, was welcome to attend. This was devastating to Claudia as she considered this woman to be her mother too. This rejection was another reminder to her that she didn't belong.

Dear Reno.

Please advise me what to do about this perdicament I got myself involed in.

I am all shaken up about it, do you remember in one of my letters to you, about the Blonde I have been going with the one who just got out of jail well the cops have their eye on him suppose they pick him up, and question him, about what he has been doing, and who has he been hanging around with could he prove that he slept at my house, and had sex with him for one week streight please Reno tell me what to do I have been very nervous since I heard all about this I am so scared I might go to jail, could they actually prove anything maybe they might take his word against mine being that I am a fag and well known, in nat vernos.

Please answer this letter as quickly as possible I am waiting patiently for your reply I can't write anymore because

I am so upset about this
whole deal. I am trying
to get some loot as fast as
possible so I could get to
you as fast as I could I
want to leave as soon as possible
the fare is only $50.63 by
train, I hope I could get it
fast, If I get it I'll leave

before the holidays I can't
wait any longer to get out
of Mt Vernon, to much has
been happening to me I
am getting to be to well
known, I can't take it much
longer, now with this other
scene I ~~don't~~ have to leave.
So Reno write, and let me
know what you think about
this whole scene, I am
desperate waiting. For your
answer, So long.

P.S.
love + kisses
+ + + + + x

P.P.S.
"HURRY UP"

Your friend
always
Charlie

Dear Reno

Please advise me what to do about this predicament I got myself involved in.

I'm all shaken up about it, do you remember in one of my letters to you, about the blonde I have been going with the one who just got out of jail well the cops have their eye on him, suppose they pick him up, and question him about what he has been doing, and who he has been hanging around with could he prove that he slept at my house, and had sex with him for one week straight please Reno tell me what to do I have been very nervous since I heard all about this I am so scared I might go to jail, could they actually prove anything maybe they might take his word against mine being that I am a fag, and well known in Mt Vernon.

"Please" answer this letter as quickly as possible I am waiting patiently for your reply I can't write anymore because I'm so upset about this whole deal. I am trying to get some loot as fast as possible so I could get to you as fast as I could I want to leave as soon as possible the fare is only $50.63 by train, I hope I could get it fast, if I get it I'll leave before the holidays I can't wait any longer to get out of Mt Vernon, to much has been happening to me I am getting to be to well known, I can't take it much longer, know with this other scene I have to leave. So Reno write, and let me know what you think about this whole scene, I am desperate waiting for your answer. So long.

Your friend always Charlie.

Charlie, perhaps the most outward, energetic, disorderly, and unapologetic queen, was never found.

Robert Rossi
5 So. Oxford St
Bklyn, N.Y.

Dear Keno;

Well I went to the halloween
ball last week at the Hotel
Mc Alpin with Georgie Wolf Girl
and Mascari.

Well the queens all looked
horrid. Only Cygroun and
Nickolena looked good.

Tony L. had Lavender Hair and
she was a scream she looked
everything but Marilyn Monroe
and Klaivra the fat cow looked
terrible she was so fat, she
peed in a piss bowl, I had to
pull her out, she is so fat.

Pretty boy Johnny looked beautiful
but the dress was from nowhere
nowhere. It was really a
faccia drag.

Dear Reno,

Well I went to the Halloween Ball last week at the Hotel McAlpin with Georgie Well the Queens all looked horrid. Only Carmen and Nickolena looked good. Tony L had lavender hair and she was a scream she looks everything but Marilyn Monroe. And Kaivra the fat cow looks terrible she was so fat. She fell in a piss bowl I had to pull her out. She is so fat.

Pretty boy Johnny looks beautiful, but the dress was from numbers know where. It was really a faccia drag. I'm going to

New Jersey Monday to look for work. Well the Gavone that broke Algene's nose was an fresh rube that I knew. He is in jail for hitting a queen on 42nd St. He really is a lovely boy. Well tonight will be Sat. nite and as usual Sat is a bummish nite for trade so I must be sure to dash. Well that's all for now.

Gigi

GiGi was never found. Daphne shared with me, she is believed to be dead.

almost every day for a
week before you left but
never could get you home
I know you also tried to
get me, but I've really
been busy with my job
& apt. It's been tough for
me these last 2 weeks with
all the borrowing I've done
I hope I can get on my feet
again in the next 2 weeks.

Pleas write me soon &
I'll try to spend a
weekend with you. How is
your new apt.? Are you
coming to the city on weekends? Write & dish me all
the dirt.

How you like your job? Trade
it.

Your friend Amy - Billie

March 30, 1955

Dear Reno,

Please forgive me for writing this in pencil, but I'm at my new place and didn't even have writing papers.

I am very happy to hear that you are working. I am only sorry I did not get to see you off before you left.

I've been calling you almost every day for a week before you left but never could get you home. I know you also tried to get me, but I've really been busy with my job and apartment.

Please write me soon and I'll try to spend a weekend with you. How is your new apartment? Are you coming to the city on weekends? Write and dish me all the dirt. How you like your new job? Trade? Etc.

Your friend always Billie

Billy "Billie Baker" Norton used his talents to find his purpose and was rising to prominence as a successful fashion designer during the 60s and 70s. Unfortunately, like so many men during the 1980s, he contracted HIV. When he told his partner he had found out he was positive, the young man walked into the kitchen, pulled a knife out of the drawer and stabbed Billy to death.

a wild time, saw Amber & Jackie and that crowd, they have a home there. Teri and Billy didn't take one this year.

I am still working for Teri, but I don't know for how long, my hand are still broken out, he been to a couple of Doctors, and was told I might have to give up Hairdressing, I tried everything, like wearing gloves, but nothing seem to help.

Everything is just about the same here,

I guess you know that Charly moved, his new address is 346. NO. High St, he have a nice two room apt, his still his same old self. I see him quite often in Ross's bar. while jumpson a Wed, night.

Gene, Ray and Vonnie are leaving for P. R. this week, I hardly ever see Ray, I guess you know about little Bobby by now his very bad off again.

I ran into Billy Baker about a month ago, he was leaving for Europe in a few days,

I also heard a dish about Jan — Josephine having a fight in a bar and Jan, having this number beat Baker up.

Well, Ed. I guess you really love Calif. and Id. love to make it out to see you, well someday,

Miss you very much,

Your Friend,
Joe.

August 1, 1965

Hi Ed,

Hope everything is O.K. with you, sorry its taken me so long to answer your letter.

I was on vacation for the 1st two weeks in July, I went to Mrytle Beach So. Carolina for one week, and had a ball. Ed its fabulous out there never have I seen so many gorgeous numbers, I had a few scenes, Last weekend I went to Fire Island with Tony + Billy had a wild time, saw Amber + Jackie and that crowd, they have a house there. Teri and Billy didn't take one this year.

I am still working for Teri, but I don't know for how long, my hands are still broken out, I've been to a couple doctors, and was told I might have to giving up hairdressing, I tried everything, like creamy gloves, but nothing seems to help.

Everything is just about the same here, I guess you know that Charley moved, his new address is 346 No. High St., he has a nice two room apt, he's still his same old self. I see him quite often in Rose's Bar, where jumps on a Wednesday night. Gene, Raj and Vinnie are leaving for P.R. this week, I hardly ever see Raj, I guess you know about little Bobby by now he's very bad off again. I ran into Billy Baker about a month ago, he was leaving for Europe in a few days.

I also heard a dish about Jan – Josephine having a fight in a bar and Jan, having this number beat Baker up.

Well, Ed, I guess you really love Calif. and I'd love to make it out to see you, well someday.

Miss you very much, Your Friend, Joe

The final letter in the collection is from Joe. He opens the letter using Reno's real name, Ed, the only person to do so in all the correspondence. It is written seven years after his previous, which was penned in 1958. Joe was thirty-two or thirty-three years old and he recaps where the Boomatzas are. Some have moved on and some are in the exact same place, but the circle is broken. There is a sense of sadness and a longing for the old days, but Joe had moved on in search of himself. The remaining queens were fond of him and shared with me all they could remember, which helped me fill in the missing pieces and further helped me to understand his relationship with Reno. Joe was the silent observer who stood on the edge of the group looking in, never bringing too much attention to himself. I picture him in his car, driving off into the sunset. Joe "the Beak" was never found.

Henry "Adrian" Arango, who stripped as Salome at the 82 Club, is the oldest living drag queen in New York City. Well into his nineties, Adrian still does drag! He is an active member of the community and proudly continues to work in the costume department at the Metropolitan Opera House as a seamster with the union.

On his journey, he met a wonderful man and fell in love. They were married and spent several years together in harmony before his husband passed. Adrian lives in the home the two purchased together in Queens with his beloved husband's ex-wife and children. "We're not your typical family—but we are a family all the same," he told me with a smile.

Terry "Teri" Noel, the beautiful chorus girl, said her goodbyes and left the 82 Club to enjoy a full-time accounting job. And when it comes to weighing risk against reward there is no better example than Terry Noel. The tremendous risks Terry took during her transition resulted in the ultimate reward; to thrive as the happy, well-adjusted fully realized woman she always knew herself to be. Terry was able to fully assimilate into the world with her identity confirmed and no longer questioned by her or anyone else.

Her mother became a tremendous support and helped Terry finance her second SRS revision surgery. She helped secure Terry's gender changes for all her legal documents. In 1968 Terry's mother paved the way for further acceptance by bringing Terry home to meet the extended family as the daughter she was very proud of. A year later, Terry went on to meet and then marry the man she fell in love with and adopted his young son as her own. It was a bond that was forged in love from the start and only grew stronger over fourteen years until it came to an amicable close. It was during her marriage that she began her career at one of the most high-level national security departments in Virginia performing data entry. After twenty-five years at the agency Terry retired, feeling very fulfilled in her career and personal life. Terry shares that it was always her greatest wish, post-transition, to lead an ordinary life. Well, let's just say there is nothing ordinary about this extraordinary woman and trailblazer.

Anyone who decides to embark on gender transition today is presented with an insurmountable set of challenges each step of the way. Terry, undergoing this at the vanguard with little-to-no resources, is a true pioneer. Her determination allowed her to survive an uncharted but necessary journey to find her true self on the other side. The moral panic that exists now around trans people relies on a belief that trans identities are new, "woke" fads. Of course, we know this to be untrue—that even ancient societies and cultures held space for individuals to exist outside of the binary, or to move within it. Terry Noel is part of that proud legacy, but her fearlessness is something we can all aspire to.

Robin "Stacy Morgan" Tyler, who performed at the 82 Club as Judy Garland, continues a legacy of lifelong LGBTQ+ activism, as an agent for change and a force to be reckoned with.

Robin explained to me, "I was there on the second night of the Stonewall uprisings in 1969 but remained on the sidelines for fear of being deported." Even though she didn't fight on that night, a decision she regrets, Robin has been fighting ever since. Through the 1970s Robin honed her voice and platform as one of the first out lesbian stand-up comics with a decidedly political slant. Robin recounted that her early training at the 82 Club prepared her for dealing with hecklers. When an inebriated male patron blurted out, "Are you a lesbian?" she shot back, "Are you the alternative?!"

As a national event coordinator for close to thirty years, in 1979 Robin organized the historic National March on Washington for

Lesbian and Gay Rights, drawing over 100,000 protestors to the capital, and again in 1987 where the AIDS quilt was unfurled and on full display for the first time. As the fight for marriage equality began to gain momentum Robin and her partner, Diane Olson, filed California's first lawsuit for marriage equality rights in February 2004. As a result of their continuous work and perseverance, they were included in the first group of couples to be officially married in June 2008 when the California Supreme Court legalized same-sex marriage. Now into her eighties, Robin continues to challenge the status quo and make her voice heard; a voice she found on the fateful night in 1969 at the Stonewall Inn.

Dear Reno,

    I was a little disappointed that you decided to stay in New Orleans indefinitely.
Have you changed your mind yet? If youre really having a ball with that new lover and all,
I can see your point. But I'd still like to see you back home in Mount Vernon. Lately thing
have been just too bunny around here lately. I never made the Cork scene this Saturday.
I heard it was the end. I made my usual appearance at the 415, with intentions of later
flying to the cork. I met these four ballet danders. Two girls, (real). And two Nens.
The girls were two of the most gorgeous fish I've ever seenn. One looked like Loretta Young
young, and the other was a cross between Ava and Pier Angeli. Gorgeous. I sat at there
table. They dug me. (I was Painted! Shocked?) Later that evening a gorgeous, but
gorgeous blond came in with a cute little nen and were seated next to us. The blond was
straight and dug the Loretta Young fish demently. (The both girls had the most stunning
bodies I've ever seenn. They looked like real Live models of the "Billie Baker Bodies".
To make a long story short, the blond and his friend invited all of us to their "apartment"
after the bar closed. When I saw him, I forgot all about the Cork. He xx had his eye on
the fish all along. It turned out the "apartment was a suite of rooms at the Madison Hotel.
Madison Avenue and 58th St. The little cute nen with him was slightly loaded. His father
owns much horse stables. There were many pictures of Horses all over the walls. The place
itself was fabulous. And guess xhax who lived next door? Joe Di Maggio. Gay?
    After we got there, we did much dancing for about two hours. I was cruising the
blonde, he was cruising the fish, the nens were cruising the blonde, the little nen was
cruising everybody, the Ava cunt was cruising me, and all of a sudden another number came
out of one of the bedrooms and xixxixix joined the Cruise of the Year. The outcome was
next. The scene was off with the fish. They cracked when the numbers p came right out and
propositioned them. Then they flew with the nens. Daphne is left alone with the three
numbers. They were all the type that I'm batz, over. They looked like College Connecticut
numbers. They were very annoyed that the cunts flew. And even less annoyed with Daphne
boomatza. I pulled all kinds of scens to get them to dig my charms. They were'nt annoyed
All of a sudden, one of them opens this huge floor to ceiling window. It was freezing out.
"Here's where Baphne gets thrown out I thought?" But they were'nt evil. Just bugged. I
made my apoligies, and flew. They were leaving town the next morning. I told them, if they
ever wanted to xxdx see my painted face again, they would know where to find me. I was
supposed to go down the 415 last night (Wednesday) to meet the fish again.   I got hung
up with my Astoria lover instead. He still digs me demently. He's so sweet, but I don't
get the same king of a demented feeling that he gets for me. Mary, he worships the ground
I walk on. I really feel sorry for him. I'd never be able to say anything to hurt him.
He's one of these numbers that would be likely to do the gas pipe scene if I did.

from letter dated February 13, 1958

I was a little disappointed that you decided to stay in New Orleans
indefinitely. Have you changed your mind yet? If youre really
having a ball with that new lover and all, I can see your point. But
I'd still like to see you back home in Mount Vernon.

Michael "Daphne" Alogna became a playwright, performer and
puppeteer at the Marionette Puppet Theater, in Central Park. He
became the beloved artistic director and proudly ran the famous
Puppet Theater for over thirty years, entertaining generations of
children and adults until he retired. During this period Daphne
found the love she had been seeking and it turned out she didn't
have to look very far, as he lived right in her neighborhood. Aaron

was a male model in New York. When they met, Aaron was an addict and Daphne helped to get him clean and off drugs. They were happy together for over eighteen years before Aaron passed away due to complications from HIV. He loved and adored Daphne and encouraged all the drag, because Aaron enjoyed nothing more than watching Daphne shine. Daphne passed away during the world coronavirus pandemic of 2020.

The ability for LGBTQ+ people to survive during the ultraconservative, pre-Stonewall era of 1950s America was challenging. Living their truth as a gay Americans came at a tremendous cost, and the struggles they had to endure in the face of adversity is heartbreaking. Though their situations and paths varied greatly, each faced their respective path with the conviction and tenacity of true survivors, no matter the odds.

CHAPTER TWELVE

Thriving

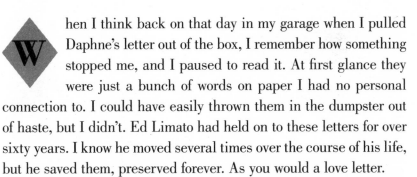

hen I think back on that day in my garage when I pulled Daphne's letter out of the box, I remember how something stopped me, and I paused to read it. At first glance they were just a bunch of words on paper I had no personal connection to. I could have easily thrown them in the dumpster out of haste, but I didn't. Ed Limato had held on to these letters for over sixty years. I know he moved several times over the course of his life, but he saved them, preserved forever. As you would a love letter.

These letters flung open the door and allowed me to enter a world I knew nothing about. They challenged me to seek information about the past, with the hope of understanding our queer history. I can't imagine Ed held onto them for the same reason.

So why did he? I have asked myself that question a thousand times, trying to unravel this mystery and I believe I now understand my own question. Ed was a smart man and I believe he felt that if he hadn't made the change and left his community of friends, his dreams of success would have been harder to achieve. To do that, he had to make a choice and leave the familiar world behind.

In time, he began to grow beyond his friends. I don't feel this was a calculated move, it was more likely a natural progression. Time determines all and sometimes people just stop sharing the same interests which results in ultimately growing apart.

This would have been around the period Ed was becoming a talent manager in New York. Due to discrimination and the stigma in the job market against homosexuals Ed had to hide his sexuality in his chosen profession by appearing straight. He had to be conscious of his masculinity. My theory is not too far out there, because this idea of code-switching is something every queer person alive has done or must do at some point—hide who they really are and appear more palatable to straight society. This is done for survival to blend in. Ed became all about his career and he would let nothing get in the way of that. He was ambitious and in the early years of his career he wasn't going to allow his sexuality to interfere.

Ed never forgot his friends. He couldn't if he tried. He surrounded himself with people who had a little "extra" going on. He was drawn to intriguing people who sparked his interest which is evident by the mega-stars he discovered and represented throughout his successful career as a talent agent in Hollywood. The Boomatzas had this quality too, they were edgy and controversial and looked at the world through a different lens, giving each other the courage to exist. They were all ahead of their time. The Boomatzas had been at the beginning of Ed's journey and he held on to these letters as a reminder of their collective past. Plausibly, the Ed I knew may have been harboring guilt for his success in life and self-reproach for losing touch and moving on leaving his friends behind. These feelings were personal to him as young Reno Martin and to the man he became.

For many years, the mere mention of drag was off the table, Ed's performed masculinity getting the better of him. Near the end of

Ed's life, though, there was a
time my partner Richard and I
were with him for a long weekend at one of his homes in Palm
Springs. This house was a mid-
century modern fantasy; quite
spectacular! One afternoon Ed
was playing Shirley Bassey loud
through his speaker system just
as I was coming out of the pool.
Shirley was belting out "I'm

coming up so you better get this party started . . ."

Overtaken by the music and feeling inspired, I grabbed a large
pool towel, whipped it around my body like a gown and began my
dramatic entrance down the steps and into the sunken living room,
lip synching in perfect unison to Ms. Bassey's iconic voice.

Suddenly Ed's voice cried out, "STOP!" He reached over and
turned off the music. "Stop what you are doing right now!" his boom-
ing voice filled the room. Then he leaned over, flicked on the music
and shouted, "Go back, and take it from the top!"

Something in Ed had softened and changed. The wall he had built
up against his perception of drag had vanished. In that moment,
toward the end of his life, he made peace with his past and started
to accept femininity again, instead of vilifying it in himself and the
people he knew. From then on, he encouraged me to do drag. He
wanted me to do drag! Ed would tell Robbie and I we should dress
up as the Dolly Sisters—of course, we had no idea who the Dolly
Sisters were. Not a problem—Ed educated us.

"Craigy, I want you and Robbie to be Marilyn Monroe and Jane
Russell. You'd be perfect!" This idea was announced as though he
alone had discovered the art form.

Ed's acceptance of my drag and his endorsement was important to
me because he mattered to me, and I looked up to him. When I reflect
on the early days, when Robbie and I started experimenting with drag

as young men, we didn't know why we had a desire to do it. Of course, it was fun to turn heads and get any attention (good or bad), but we did it for ourselves. Now, after discovering the letters and learning of their historical importance, as well as meeting these amazing pioneers from that time in history, presenting in drag goes beyond what I show on the outside—for me it has become more internal. I do drag, not because I want to, but because I have to. It is my art and I like to believe in some small way is my contribution to our history.

When you give up your gender role and step out as a self-created female illusion of yourself, you discover something within, and that feeling can be extremely powerful. Pushing boundaries and allowing yourself to be seen through transformation—letting others be entertained and inspired—can have life-changing impact. To be able to say something and to speak to someone through art either theatrically or politically is what a drag queen aspires to do and by understanding this, transformation and illusion take on a deeper personal meaning. The fact that performative drag has reached the "mainstream" through competition reality shows, TV series and film is nothing short of extraordinary when considering the past. Today, when we think about a drag queen, chances are it's a professional performer who has created a bigger-than-life persona to inhabit over-the-top costumes rooted in artifice, and exaggeration.

But in today's world, drag has evolved from the traditional confines of female illusionist to a much broader form of personal artistic expression. Through our modern lens, the concept of a female illusionist or impersonator can be viewed as an historic and crucial first step in gender variant presentation. As the concept of drag has found its way into mainstream American media, the presentation of "old school" or "high femme drags" is perhaps a bit more static when compared to today's fluid interpretations of gender and non-binary expressions.

While some remain committed to the more traditional and celebrated "pageant queen" ideals others are breaking away and exploring highly individualized presentations that speak more directly to who they are and what they have to say. There is a freedom within today's drag culture, no longer awarding top honors just to the most beautiful or passable but also to the most inventive, the most daring and the most unique.

Just as there isn't one right way to be queer there's not one right way to do drag—commit and make it your own. It's a chance to try on a new persona, to challenge yourself and see where the journey takes you. It's an art form. It's transformative. It's subversive. It's powerful. It's political. Its whatever you want it to be. It's taking a risk and finding your own reward.

The fact that, as queer people in much of the world, we can walk out our front doors unbothered is a privilege, not a birth right. It may be easy to take that fact for granted, but in looking back through our history we know better, and if we even simply look at the world now, there remain countries where homosexuality is illegal, or is punishable by death. Globally, queer people are not considered as equals still, and as we witness the beginnings of LGBTQ+ rights being struck down across the United States, there's no room for complacency. Intolerance and ignorance abound, and the desire to stigmatize and silence our voices gains traction with each passing day once again.

The trailblazers, whose letters we've read and stories we've heard, were anything but complacent. While the Stonewall uprising was a seminal moment that gave birth to the LGBTQ+ civil rights movement, our pioneers, through their intimate first-hand accounts, have shown us what came before; a collective history that was once hidden in the shadows but now shines in the proud bright light of visibility and truth. While we may be separated by geography, circumstance, and many decades we stand together as unapologetic outcasts having found salvation in each other.

(P.S. BURN this letter please.)

Acknowledgments

I am overflowing with gratitude for everyone who has helped bring my vision for *P.S. Burn This Letter Please* to fruition. This journey, which began in 2014, has been a journey of self-discovery and a deeper understanding of the hidden history of the LGBTQ+ community. My gratitude goes out to all those who have contributed to this project, from the awe-inspiring Sasha Velour, to my incredible publishing team, Callum Kenny, Jon Appleton, Katya Ellis, Lucy Martin, Lucie Sharpe and Linda Silverman for this book, as well as our team behind the award-winning documentary feature film of the same name.

I want to express my immense gratitude to the letter writers, whose bravery in sharing their stories and experiences has paved the way for others to live their truth. I stand on their shoulders and will continue to pass the torch to future generations in their honor.

I also extend my thanks to our beautiful queens. Your courage and authenticity is a shining light to us all. A heartfelt thank you goes to Henry Arango, Michael Alogna, Claude Diaz, Terry Noel, Robin Tyler, Robert Bouvard, James Bidgood, George Roth, Dayzee Dee, Veronica Nash, Maureen Corbin, and Robbie Laughlin-Bernstein for their contributions and impact on the community.

I would like to thank Esther Newton, George Chauncy, Robert J. Corber, Jeffery Escoffier, Michael Henry Adams, and Joe E. Jeffreys, whose works on queer culture and history have been instrumental in adding depth and insight to the story. Their contributions are truly appreciated.

Thank you to Billy Weiner, my creative partner. Our journey writing together will always be cherished, and even though you are no longer with us, I could feel your presence guiding me with every word I wrote. Your impact on my life and work will never be forgotten.

To my soulmate, Richard "Richie" Konigsberg, thank you for your unwavering support and encouragement throughout our many years together. Your belief in my creativity has allowed me to soar beyond my own expectations. I am forever grateful for the love and light you bring into my life.

Lastly, a heartfelt thank you to Edward F. Limato for preserving these letters and holding on to the key allowing us to unlock a piece of history that will continue to inspire and educate future generations. Your continued legacy through your foundation, supporting LGBTQ+ causes, is a testament to your selflessness and unwavering commitment to making a positive impact in the world. I miss you deeply, my dear friend.

Craig Olsen is an artist, actor, film producer and designer. He gained recognition for producing the award-winning documentary film *P.S. Burn This Letter Please*. Currently, Craig is focused on preserving LGBTQ+ history through philanthropy and education. He lives in Los Angeles with his partner, Richie Konigsberg, and their beloved chihuahuas, Oliver and Oona.